YOU'RE HIRED! GRADUATE CAREER HANDBOOK

MAXIMISE YOUR EMPLOYABILITY AND GET A GRADUATE JOB

YOU'RE HIRED! GUIDES

See our website at www.trotman.co.uk for a comprehensive list of published and forthcoming Trotman titles.

YOU'RE HIRED! GRADUATE CAREER HANDBOOK

MAXIMISE YOUR EMPLOYABILITY AND GET A GRADUATE JOB

TRISTRAM HOOLEY AND KORIN GRANT

You're Hired! Graduate Career Handbook: Maximise your employability and get a graduate job

This first edition published in 2017 by Trotman Publishing, a division of Crimson Publishing Ltd., 19–21c Charles Street, Bath BA1 1HX

© Crimson Publishing 2017

Authors Tristram Hooley and Korin Grant

British Library Cataloguing in Publication Data
A catalogue record for this book is available from the British Library

ISBN 978 1 84455 648 9

Please note that all websites given in this book are subject to change so you may find that some of these sites in time may be renamed, merge with other sites or disappear.

Designed by Nicki Averill
Typeset by IDSUK (DataConnection) Ltd
Printed and bound in Malta by Gutenberg Press Ltd, Malta

CONTENTS

ABOUT THE AUTHORS

Neither of the authors found a graduate job straight out of university. They don't regret this, but that doesn't mean that they wouldn't have liked some more advice a bit earlier. They have both had complex and chaotic careers and have spent much of their lives trying to understand how the graduate labour market works and to help current students to find a career path that works for them.

The authors worked together for a while at the University of Leicester, helping graduates to develop their careers. They didn't always agree then and they certainly don't always agree now. Nonetheless, they have written, rewritten, edited and re-edited all of the chapters of this book until they are sure that this book contains the distilled wisdom of over 30 years of careers work with graduates.

They hope that this book will be useful to a new generation of students and graduates.

Tristram Hooley has a complex working life. He is variously the Director of Research at The Careers & Enterprise Company, Professor of Career Education at the University of Derby and a professor at the Inland Norway University of Applied Science. This means that he spends a lot of time on trains and planes, which gives him a lot of time to think and write about careers. He has published over a 100 books, papers and articles on careers and related subjects, including *You're Hired: Job Hunting Online*. He is also the author of the Adventures in Career Development blog (https://adventuresincareerdevelopment.wordpress.com).

Korin Grant has recently joined Loughborough University in the role of Postgraduate Careers Consultant. Previously to this she worked for 15 years at the University of Leicester in various student-facing careers-related roles. These included leading on employability awards, managing placement schemes and helping students to make effective transitions from school to university and then on to graduate work or study. She really, really likes helping students and seeing them go on to enjoy their next step in life.

ACKNOWLEDGEMENTS

Thanks are due to Freya and Reuben for allowing us to write this book.

We'd also like to thank Della Oliver for all of her help, advice and support in putting the book together.

WHO IS THIS BOOK FOR?

This is a book for current students and new graduates.

In the ideal world you would buy this book as you pack your bags for your first term at university. You would then refer to it often and use it to guide your career development throughout your period at university and your first couple of years after you graduate. In this ideal world you would take the book with you on work experience placements and periods of study abroad and always be thinking about the skills that you are developing and how they might inform your later career.

Back in reality we realise that you are probably buying this the day after the graduation ball. You have partied too much, studied too little and given no attention to finding a job. Now your parents are screaming at you and you've got no idea where to start. Thankfully, you've now got your hands on this book!

This book is for people at both ends of these extremes, the planners and the partiers, the CV junkies and those who never thought that university would end. It is also for those in the middle and in the middle of their degrees who are just starting to worry.

Depending on who you are, you might read this book differently. If you start with the Introduction we'll try to direct you straight to the bit that you need most.

A NOTE ON THE USE OF URLS, REFERENCES AND EXAMPLES

We have used a lot of websites to help us to write this book. We felt that some of them were so useful that they might be worth you having a look at them as well. We've tried to give simple URLs that you can easily type into your browser.

However, the web is changing all the time. If you visit a weblink and find that it has changed or gone, then we apologise. We'd suggest that you put the title of the web page into Google and see if you can find where it has gone. If you still can't find it DON'T PANIC, no one weblink is critical. There are plenty more websites out there.

Most of this book is based on our experience. It isn't an academic book and so we didn't want to fill it up with references. But where we say something that we feel needs to be backed up we have included an endnote. If you are interested, just flip to the back of the book and you will find the full reference. If you aren't too interested in these references, then just ignore the endnotes altogether.

Finally, we have written a lot of case studies and examples. Most of these are based on our experience of the situations that students and graduates find themselves in. We've tried to make them as true and accurate as possible, but the graduate labour market is complex and always changing. So, it is always important to do your own research to supplement the examples and tips that we give you.

INTRODUCTION

University is one of the great adventures of your life. It will challenge you and stretch you in a whole host of ways. You'll meet new people, learn new skills, discover new facts and have some fantastic opportunities. University is also a time in many people's lives when they make a new, and often lifelong, circle of friends, meet their partner and learn a lot about themselves. Alongside all of this you'll be having a social life, going to parties, playing sports, getting political, staying up late and debating life, the universe and everything.

So how on earth, with all of this going on, are you supposed to start worrying about your career?

In fact, you've already made a lot of really important career decisions. You've decided what subjects to study at 16 and 18 and then passed at least some of them (otherwise you wouldn't have got to university). You've then chosen a university and a subject to study. You may also have worked in some jobs, travelled, met people and taken up loads of opportunities. If you've been paying attention, all of this will have told you something about yourself, about what you like and don't like, and what you might want to do. So, you've actually been working on your career development for years (maybe without even realising it).

The point is that your career is not something that happens after you graduate. Your career has already been happening and it is continuing to happen all around you, even when you aren't thinking about it at all. Building your career is not just about finding a job, it is actually about deciding who you are and what kind of life you want to lead. This is important stuff and we think that it is worth you spending some time on it.

What this book is going to do is to help you think about what is the best thing to spend your time on.

We can't guarantee you a solid gold house or an enormous pay cheque, but we can promise that if you put in some hard work you will be able to shape your career in a way that will make you healthier, happier and probably richer.

So, are you ready to get started?

How to read this book

We have set this book out in such a way as to allow someone who has just started university to benefit from the first chapter ('I just don't know what to do with myself') to the last ('If at first you don't succeed …'). But there is no reason for you to start at page 1 and read the chapters in order. Each chapter deals with a different aspect of career development, management and job searching. Read the summaries or dip into each chapter to decide where you are right now and where you would like to start your reading.

Each chapter follows a similar structure and contains the same recurring features. You will find:

Tips – Our tips are short, simple ideas that are easy to follow up on.

Activities – Our activities will help you to engage more deeply with the topic of the chapter and will help you to apply some of the theory in a practical exercise.

Case studies – In our case studies we bring the principles of the chapter to life by telling the story of a student or recent graduate.

Would you like to … – These sections provide information about a particular career option. You will find at least one in each chapter and we hope that a couple of them may spark your interest. This isn't meant to be a comprehensive directory of graduate opportunities. If you are looking for that, try visiting Prospects (www.prospects.ac.uk) or one of the other websites that we are going to introduce you to in this book.

What is in this book?

Each of the chapters is outlined below. Read through and highlight the chapters that you feel pertain to you and your situation. You can go from start to finish or pick a chapter in the middle of the book.

1. **I just don't know what to do with myself** This chapter will encourage you to reflect on your values, likes and strengths. It will show how these attributes can help to identify career paths.

Read this chapter if:

■ you are not sure what you want to do after your degree or even how to begin thinking about a career

■ you find yourself at a crossroads in your career – perhaps you feel as if you've studied the wrong degree or you are unhappy with your first graduate role.

2. **Making the most of your degree** Whether you are doing a vocational or non-vocational degree, you still need to think about the relationship between your learning and your career. This chapter will help you to think about the subject you are studying and how this might be useful to you when you graduate.

Read this chapter if:

■ you are not sure how to talk about what you have learned in your degree

■ you are not sure what transferrable skills you have developed through your studies

■ you are wondering if there was any point in undertaking a degree.

3. **Are you experienced?** There are many different ways in which you can gain experience and develop yourself while you are at university. This chapter will discuss volunteering, part-time working, work experience, placements and study abroad. It will show you how to make the most of each of these opportunities.

Read this chapter if:

■ you aren't sure what should be included in the 'work experience' section of your CV

■ you don't know if you have any relevant work experience

■ you would like to get more work experience.

4. **It's not what you know, it's who you know** Networks are critical to finding employment. As a student and recent graduate you will have opportunities to build your networks, but who is it best to connect with and how should you do this?

Read this chapter if:

■ the idea of 'networking' makes you feel nervous

■ you don't know who to network with or why

■ you are not sure what your networks have to do with getting a job

■ you want to build up your network.

5. **Look before you leap** Researching possible jobs, careers and employers can help you to make decisions about your career and give you the edge. This chapter will set out practical tips for identifying opportunities and gaining insights.

   Read this chapter if:

   ■ you are applying for jobs, or have an interview or assessment centre to attend

   ■ you are wondering how to find out more about particular jobs, organisations and industries

   ■ you want to be able to compete successfully in interviews and assessment centres

   ■ you aren't sure why you need to do research.

6. **Should I stay or should I go?** Many students stay on after their first degree to do more study. Is this really a good idea? This chapter will examine whether postgraduate study will give you the edge and what course to choose.

   Read this chapter if:

   ■ you don't really understand what postgraduate study is and would like to know more about it

   ■ you are thinking about, or have already applied for, further study

   ■ you would like to know what career options postgraduate study can open up.

7. **Successful applications and interviews** This chapter will outline typical recruitment practices used by employers and provide strategies that you can use to come out on top. The chapter includes common errors made at each stage and a sample CV to help get you started.

   Read this chapter if:

   ■ you are at any stage of the application process

   ■ you feel unsure about what to expect when you make an application

   ■ psychometric testing is getting you down

   ■ your applications are not successful and you don't know why

   ■ you think your CV needs help.

8. **Help me!** This chapter reminds you that you are not on your own. Universities provide careers services and other forms of help. How should you make the most of these? The chapter will also talk about where else you can get support, including asking your friends and family and, of course, getting on to Google.

Read this chapter if:

- you are not sure what your careers service could offer you to help you get a job
- asking for help is difficult for you
- you have a problem and you don't know where to turn.

9. **The importance of plan B** Things don't always work out. This chapter will encourage you to develop an alternative plan in case you don't get your first choice.

Read this chapter if:

- your career path is looking unsure
- you want to develop a 'plan B'.

10. **Starting work** Getting a job is only the start of having a successful career. This chapter will help you to think about making a good impression when you first start work. It will cover office politics, dress codes and getting through the first month.

Read this chapter if:

- you are starting a new job or placement
- you are leaving your first job
- you want some tips on making a good impression at work.

11. **If at first you don't succeed ...** Sometimes jobs aren't what you expect. Other times graduates may find themselves in jobs that they never wanted in the first place. This chapter will discuss making the best of things, job crafting, moving on and starting over.

Read this chapter if:

- your graduate role isn't what you expected
- you want to make a change
- you want to learn about crafting your own career.

Finally, in our Conclusion we leave you with some final thoughts, tips and reminders. We provide a summary of the book and our recommendations. The conclusions will leave with a handy reminder of some of our top tips for managing your graduate job search and career successfully.

Dip into the book wherever it seems you need the most help. Then dip back in again when you reach the next or a different stage of your career plan.

Happy careering!

1 I JUST DON'T KNOW WHAT TO DO WITH MYSELF

Making a decision about what to do with your life isn't easy. Many people find choosing a subject at university difficult enough. Finding a job is even more tricky, as there is so much that you don't know about what different jobs are like and which ones you will be good at.

Thinking deeply about yourself, your likes and dislikes, what you are good and bad at, and so on can be really useful. This chapter will help you to get to know yourself a bit better and then to think about what this might mean for your future career.

This chapter will help you to:

■ understand what you are like and why this is important to employers

■ think about your values, likes and interests

■ consider your strengths and weaknesses

■ use these reflections to help you find your career path.

Introduction

When you start thinking about your career it is really important to remember that it is YOUR career and YOUR life.

You may have found yourself at university studying a subject which you don't find interesting, which your parents pushed you into or which you thought was going to be completely different. On the other hand, you might love your subject and want to spend the rest of your life pursuing palaeontology, art history or education. Other people may have found that the academic part of university is nothing special but they really come into their own when they are DJ-ing in the student bar, running a political campaign or organising the RAG society.

How you spend your time at university, what you like and dislike, probably gives you a lot of clues about your career. That is why it is worth your spending some time thinking about who you are, what you like and what you want from your life.

Your first job after university is an important one. It can influence the direction of the rest of your life. It is important that you make sure that it is the right decision for you and not just what your mum, friends or lecturers expect you to do.

This is why we are going to be pushing you to spend some time reflecting on yourself.

What is reflection?

Reflection is about holding up a mirror to have a look at yourself. You already know what your face looks like, but you still use a mirror every time you go out. Mainly, looking at yourself just tells you what you already know, but sometimes you see something new. Perhaps this is because you have changed – or perhaps it is because you are looking at yourself from a different angle.

It is pretty easy to hold up a mirror to look at your face, but this doesn't tell you much about what you are really like. This is why we are encouraging you to get into the habit of thinking about your personality, skills and interests. This kind of reflection can be really useful in helping you to decide on your career direction. Reflection is not a one-off activity. You wouldn't think that looking at yourself in the mirror on Wednesday means that you are ready to go out on Friday. You have to keep reflecting on yourself all the time. Every activity that you do gives you more material to reflect on. Perhaps you have just finished a module on statistics or spent time producing a leaflet for the Chess Society. Did you like it? What skills did it use? Were you good at it? Could you get better? Would you like to do more of it? Try getting into the habit of asking yourself these kinds of questions.

Reflection is not just something that you do in private! Employers will ask you to reflect when you fill in an application form or attend an interview. Most applications will include a personal statement. In essence this is just a piece of reflection written down. The trick in presenting your reflections for others is to highlight your strengths without looking as if you are boasting. Many employers will consider reflection to be an important employability skill and will be looking for you to provide evidence that you can think about your strengths and weaknesses and demonstrate that you can learn from your mistakes.

CASE STUDY

Jim knows that he is brilliant at everything. Top of his class at school, captain of the rugby team, popular with everyone in his year at university and ready to move into a high-powered career in corporate law.

When it is time to apply for graduate schemes Jim rolls up his sleeves and starts typing …

He finds it a bit more difficult than he thought. He's done lots of things, but which ones should he tell the company that he wants to work for about? In the end he decides to list his achievements, telling them about everything from his first swimming certificate to his GCSEs to his runner-up medal for the Varsity Rugby Cup. He reviews the application, is sure that he is, indeed, awesome and clicks send.

…

Sue is reviewing graduate applications for Law Co. She comes across one from Jim. He meets all of the criteria: good A levels, studying law at a good university, lots of extra-curricular activities. But his application doesn't really tell her anything about who he really is. It is impossible to work out why he wants to work here, whether he would be any good at the job and what he has learned from being involved in so many activities. She is really looking for someone who can communicate their strengths and weaknesses and provide evidence that they will be able to learn once they start work.

Jim's application goes onto the REJECT pile.

Knowing yourself

It's not always easy know yourself. You are complicated and changing all the time. What is more, the way that you see yourself is different to how others see you.

The former U.S. Secretary of Defense Donald Rumsfeld has become famous for his comment that:

> *As we know, there are known knowns; there are things we know we know. We also know there are known unknowns; that is to say we know there are some things we do not know. But there are also unknown unknowns – the ones we don't know we don't know. And if one looks throughout the history of our country and other free countries, it is the latter category that tend to be the difficult ones.*[i]

At first reading this might seem to be complete gibberish. But, if you think about it, it starts to make sense (we promise!). You know what you know and you know what you don't know, but what about what you don't know you don't know? This might be a bit clearer if we draw this as a table:

What everyone knows about you	What other people know about you (but you don't)
What only you know about you	What no-one knows about you (including yourself!)

Everyone knows that you are a brilliant singer because you are always performing in your band. They understand that you are outgoing, confident and good at performing.

Only you know about your secret hobby of building model airplanes. You keep it secret because you think that it is a bit embarrassing, but it shows that you have a fantastic eye for detail and a lot of patience.

Your manager at your part-time job knows that you are good at solving problems. She notices that you often come up with creative solutions that others might not. It's one of the reasons she often asks you to work during the busier shifts. Your manager has never thought to mention it to you as she assumes that you are aware of this.

There may be plenty of things that no-one knows about you yet. Some of these things may be more important than others, especially when it comes to your career. How will you cope with working set hours in an office? What sort of manager would you be? Will you enjoy office parties? These questions are useful to keep in mind because they remind us that (1) there are some things we still don't know about ourselves and (2) our character is not fixed; there will always be more to know and learn about ourselves.

Knowing yourself

If you were to complete this table above for yourself, what would you include? Who else might you ask to help you complete the table?

What does everyone know about you?

What do only you know about you?

What do you think other people know about you?

What does nobody know about you?

Testing your personality

You can also use personality tests to help you to figure out what you are like. These types of tests are often useful to get you thinking. You should be fairly sceptical if anyone tells you that a test can sum up your personality and tell you what job you should do.

Trying to measure or define your personality can seem impossible. After all, you are different when you are with your friends to how you are when you are with your parents; you are different in the morning to in the evening; and different again when you are concentrating on an essay or taking part in a discussion. However, tell someone that they are 'the kind of person who likes to follow rather than lead' and they will usually have an instinctive response to this based on their experience to date. It is by using these kinds of questions that psychologists try to build up a picture of someone's personality.

One of the approaches that psychologists use is to describe you in relation to five aspects of your personality. This is often called the Big Five and is sometimes described using the acronym OCEAN.

The Big Five or OCEAN

- **Openness to experience** describes your intellectual curiosity, creativity and preference for novelty and variety. People with high openness can be seen as adventurous but unpredictable, while those with low openness can be seen as pragmatic but closed-minded.
- **Conscientiousness** describes your tendency to be organised and dependable. If you have high conscientiousness you can come across as reliable but a bit obsessive. On the other hand, having low conscientiousness might mean that you are seen as spontaneous but not someone whom others should rely on.
- **Extroversion** describes how outgoing and sociable you are. Very extroverted people are the life and soul of the party, but can be seen as desperate for attention. Less extroverted people are more reserved and this can sometimes be perceived as being unfriendly.
- **Agreeableness** describes your tendency to be caring and cooperative and to want to get along with others. The very agreeable are nice people, but they can seem a little naive. But those with low agreeableness can be competitive, challenging and argumentative.
- **Neuroticism** describes how you deal with difficult emotions. People with a high degree of neuroticism can be dynamic but a bit unstable, while those with low neuroticism can be seen as calm but less inspiring individuals.

There are lots of ways in which you can get access to a personality test that is based on the Big Five, e.g. www.personalitytest.org.uk. However, it is always worth thinking about how reliable these tests are. There are millions of tests online that purport to describe your personality. Some of them are based on science while others are complete nonsense. If in doubt investigate who is providing you with this test and why. If it is a researcher from a university who is going to use your data in their research you are probably OK (but we would say that, wouldn't we!). If it is a cult promising that their personality test will make you a better person you might want to steer clear.

If you talk to psychologists about personality testing they will urge caution. Most will say that tests need to be used carefully and interpreted by professionals. We think that there is some value in taking some of the tests that you find online, but don't get carried away. Tests are just one tool that you can use in your reflection about yourself and your career.

The Big Five (OCEAN)

Spend a bit of time thinking about yourself in relation to the Big Five. Where would you rate yourself in relation to each of these traits? If you are feeling brave you might want to ask someone who knows you well to rate you too. Do they agree with you?

Openness to experience

Conscientiousness

Extroversion

Agreeableness

Neuroticism

Another good reason to know yourself well and to get some experience of personality tests is that many employers use these kinds of tests as part of recruitment processes or to identify gaps or training needs in their workforce. Reflecting on your personality and trying out a few tests will mean that you aren't surprised when you first encounter these. It will also mean that you get used to talking about the results of tests and thinking about how you manage different aspects of your personality.

For example, if you realise that you are high in neuroticism you might want to reflect on how this drives you to be more energetic, while also recognising that you might sometimes need to rein in your enthusiasm to avoid panicking your colleagues. Knowing about your personality helps you to deal with your flaws and make the most of your strong points.

This is not a perfect science – who you are today is not exactly who you will be in five years' time. But spending time considering these questions will help you to make effective choices about your career options and improve your performance in job applications and interviews.

TIP: EMPLOYERS' TESTS
Get familiar with some of these tests. But don't get too carried away. They are just one tool that can help you with your reflection.

Some of these tests might be used in selection procedures, while others are more usually used once you have been employed. These five tests are just the tip of the iceberg with respect to personality tests. There is a whole industry of people selling them, and then another industry of people challenging and debunking them.

Five tests that might be used by employers

Caliper Profile	An in-depth personality assessment that can be used in job matching	www.calipercorp.com
Clifton Strengthsfinder	A tool to identify your strengths and talents	www.gallupstrengthscenter. com
MBTI	A personality test that sorts you into one of 16 personality types	www.myersbriggs.org
Belbin	A test that identifies the role that you usually play in a team	www.belbin.com
16PF	A tool that is designed to reveal potential, confirm suitability for employment roles and help to identify development needs	www.16pf.com

Would you like to ... be a psychologist?

If all of this talk about testing your personality and using it to help you think about yourself and the world around you inspires you, you may be interested in considering a career as a psychologist.

Psychologists study people's behaviour, motivations, thoughts and feelings. Some work directly with people to help them overcome or control their problems, while others might be involved in developing the kinds of tests that we have discussed, working with organisations or just trying to improve our understanding of how individuals behave. There are lots of different types of psychologists and so if this job appeals to you it is worth spending some time researching the field and thinking about what aspect of it is most interesting.

This is a great job for people who have done a psychology degree, although most jobs will require you to have some additional training beyond an undergraduate degree. However, it is also possible for non-psychology graduates to take a conversion course and move into this field.

Salaries will vary greatly depending on the type of psychologist you are and the additional training you have completed, so do a bit of research to ensure that you know what to expect.

For more information about working as a psychologist see the National Careers Service job profile (http://bit.ly/2oWZfN7) or visit the British Psychological Society website (http://beta.bps.org.uk).

Values

Knowing yourself includes knowing what motivates you. What do you care about? What's important to you? When it comes to your career, your values can play a big role in the decisions you make about where to work and the kind of work you will do.

Values can be difficult to pin down. For example, ask yourself how important money is to you. Clearly, all of us need some money in return for the work that we do. Unless you are independently wealthy you need to eat, buy something to wear, pay for a roof over your head and so on. So how much money do you need? If you want to dine in Michelin-starred restaurants, walk around in Prada outfits and live in a mansion you are going to need a career that can support this kind of lifestyle.

Now ask yourself how important it is to you that your work helps people and makes the world a better place. Perhaps you are thinking about a career as an environmental campaigner, refugee worker or early years teacher. In these cases your values are leading you to a different set of careers that don't necessarily pay big bucks.

But hold on! What if you want to help people *and* wear Prada? What if you care about the world, but also want to live in a fabulous loft apartment overlooking Central Park? What if your values are in conflict with each other?

CASE STUDY

Sonam has worked hard at university to achieve an attractive profile for the top graduate recruiters. Early on in her studies she realised that she needed to achieve a decent grade (2:1, ideally) while developing transferable skills. She volunteered as a course representative and worked part time in the summers. She engaged with employers at insight days and sought out help from the careers service to make sure her applications and interviews would be strong. Sonam made sure that she made time for friends as well and kept an active social life.

As a result she is now working full time at a well-known large company. She is earning well and her colleagues are bright and enthusiastic. The office has a 'work hard, play hard' culture that should suit Sonam, given her approach to university. But it's not fun, or engaging, and she is missing her family. It doesn't seem to matter that Sonam is doing well and her manager is pleased with her work. When she goes home at night she feels unsatisfied and lonely. She hadn't realised how important it was to her that she should find her work interesting, and she hadn't thought that she would miss her family at all.

This isn't what Sonam thought a successful career would feel like.

We can all point to examples of people who seem to 'have it all', but the reality is that at different times in our lives we need to make some compromises. Early in your career search you may decide to change location, accept a lower-paid job offer or perhaps leave a comfortable job in order to get the experience you are seeking.

Your values may change at different points in your life and you may find that you are more or less willing to compromise on certain things as a result.

Exploring your values

A good exercise to try is to rate some of the following things in order of importance. It's not easy, but it can illustrate where your key values lie at the moment.

A list of career-related values

Rank	Value
	Autonomy
	Being in charge
	Being outside
	Challenging work
	Creativity
	Doing good/making a difference
	Easy work
	Home
	Learning
	Money
	People (family/friends)
	Respect
	Responsibility
	Socialising
	Time
	Travel
	Working with others
	?
	?
	?

Deciding how you rank these kinds of values is really difficult. But it can help you to build some insights about what you want, what you don't want and how you might trade one thing off against another.

Likes and interests

Knowing what you like and enjoy is an important part of making decisions about your future and career. This might seem obvious – you wouldn't embark on a career as a vet if you didn't enjoy spending time with animals – but it is sometimes hard to know where to start and how this fits in with work.

The first thing to remember is that what you like today may not be the same as what you like tomorrow. It's OK for your taste and experiences to grow and change. You've already made some decisions about what you enjoy. You have probably already chosen a place to study and an academic subject to explore. How did you make those decisions? Your experience and knowledge helped you to reach the conclusion that these were the right choices for you at this time.

Spend a few minutes thinking about things that you like about your course.

> Do you like reading/writing/doing research/speaking in class/working in a group/doing practical work/thinking about abstract theoretical ideas?

Now think about any jobs or voluntary work.

> Have you ever worked part time or full time/volunteered at school or in the community/assisted in community events or faith group activities/babysat or done odd jobs for others?

Now what about your hobbies or extra-curricular activity? What was it that made these things enjoyable?

> Do you enjoy working with others/being active and healthy/having the chance to lead/making a difference to others/seeing your ideas come to life/showing others what you can achieve?

It's also useful to remember what you have **not** enjoyed, and these things are often easier to recall. Not all unenjoyable experiences are bad (revision isn't always fun but it is a means to an end), and they can tell us a bit more about ourselves. You might remember a time when you dealt with a difficult customer as something you feel proud of or as something you'd hope not to repeat ever again.

It can be tricky to relate what you like to the world of work. Many people describe themselves as 'an avid reader', but not all of these people will become editors or authors. We're not trying to come up with a list of jobs you might enjoy but with an understanding of the types of activities that you find satisfying, interesting and fun.

Strengths and weaknesses

So far we've talked a lot about what you like, who you are and what is important to you. Of course we also need to think about what you are good at! Everybody is good at some things and less good at others. Your talents and abilities are not fixed and you will continue to learn and develop at university and beyond, but let's start with what you think you are good at now.

There may be some things that you know you are good at because you've been tested or have had successful experiences (maths, writing, looking after children, understanding scientific concepts, selling a side of fries). These are important and have probably played some part in leading you to what you are now studying for your degree.

TIP: YOU CAN LEARN!

Thinking about your strengths and weaknesses is important. A realistic assessment of what you are good at and not so good at shows self-awareness. But, remember that you can learn new things and improve in the things that you are not so good at. DON'T GIVE UP!

Remember the earlier quote from Donald Rumsfeld about known knowns and unknown knowns? This can also be applied to the different stages of ability or competence. For example, there was a time when you didn't understand algebra. You didn't know that you didn't understand it; in fact, you didn't even know it existed. Your maths teacher made you aware of algebra and you became conscious of it as a thing that you didn't understand. You began to learn how to approach algebra and with each success and each mistake you learned more until you were able to solve most algebraic questions. Now when you see '5 + X = 15' it is almost second nature to solve X. (Yes, it is 10; well done).

We've just illustrated four stages of competence:

1. unconscious incompetence: 'There is something called algebra?!'
2. conscious incompetence: 'I really don't get algebra, I keep getting the wrong answer.'
3. conscious competence: 'I've learned how to approach an algebra question.'
4. unconscious competence: 'I can do algebra in my sleep!'

So it's not always possible for you to be aware of what you are good at. Answering a question about your strengths and weaknesses will get easier with time and experience. For now it's a great idea to ask your friends and family what they think. They see you from a different perspective, and that can mean that they recognise skills that you have not noticed or perhaps not valued.

ACTIVITY 1.4

Thinking about your strengths and weaknesses

What would you list as your main strengths and abilities?

Now list your areas of weakness.

How would your friends and family view your strengths and weaknesses?

Finding your path

So, how do you put all of this together to form a meaningful vision of your future career and life?

The simple answer is that you don't. There is no crystal ball. But the answers provide important clues to the things that will help you make decisions about your future. Thinking about your values, likes, dislikes, strengths and experiences is the beginning of the process of thinking about your career.

When your values, personality traits and skills all come together in the same place (a job!) you can feel very fulfilled and satisfied. Where they are in conflict you will probably feel the need to resolve these conflicts. A job that fulfils your passion for the arts but doesn't sustain your chosen lifestyle will not last. A career that rewards you with funds for expensive holidays but leaves you bored and unchallenged will also have a shelf life.

When you are asking yourself questions try not to jump to conclusions. Reflection is a way of finding things out, but the things that you find out are not fixed.

It is perfectly normal for you to change your mind about what you want out of your work at different points in your life. You are dynamic, you can and will change at different points in your journey. This is why reflecting on what motivates you, what you enjoy and what you can do is important now and throughout your career.

Reflecting means that you can evaluate the experience that you have had (good/bad, exciting/scary) and decide how you might do things differently next time. Would you like to build on that experience or to avoid it at all costs?

Throughout this book we will come back to ideas such as values, experiences, skills and strengths. Keep your reflections in mind as you conduct research into possible career options. You have already begun making decisions about your career, possibly without giving these decisions a lot of deep thought. When the time comes to make career-related decisions (Should I apply for this internship? Do I want to attend the finance insight week? Shall I continue with my voluntary work?), you will have some basis upon which to make these decisions.

Each decision will provide you with a new experience. Continue to reflect on your experiences to help bring you closer to exciting, rewarding and meaningful opportunities.

CASE STUDY

John is an outgoing person who has always enjoyed being around people. His family and friends consider him to be an extrovert who enjoys his basketball league and is a good problem solver. When he told his parents he was joining an accountancy firm they were very surprised and wondered how he would cope. Maths had never been his strong suit!

Then John explained his role and it began to make sense. John's role at the accountancy firm is in human resources. It is John's job to find the right people for the right jobs in the company, to help new recruits settle in, train for their accreditations and solve personal issues as they arise. The job is a good one for John because it is near home, which means he can still attend his regular basketball practice. The company was able to offer a decent salary and a people-facing role that played to John's personality and strengths.

John feels that in the future he might want a more challenging role and at that point he might be willing to compromise on location or salary, but for now this role is a good match for John's values, likes and strengths.

Would you like to ... work in human resources?

Human resources professionals work in organisations to develop, advise on and implement policies relating to the effective use of staff within the organisation. Human resources professionals can take on a wide range of roles within organisations; for example, leading on issues of equality and diversity, recruitment, redeployment and redundancy and addressing strategic issues about managing talent. Entry-level roles may earn around £19,000 per year, but more experienced, better qualified and more senior roles can earn a lot more.

This job is open to all graduates, although it may particularly appeal to those who have studied social science degrees. Although it is possible to work in human resources without specific qualifications it is desirable to have a qualification from a body such as the Chartered Institute of Personnel and Development (CIPD).

Introduction

'Making the most of your degree' could be interpreted in several ways. You might be having a lot of fun at university – making lots of friends, enjoying clubs, using the gym facilities and generally having a great time. And that is an important part of making the most of your time at university. But in this chapter we want to talk about making the most of your studies and the academic subject that you have chosen.

Making the most of your degree is worth doing even if you have no interest in ever being employed. You have chosen to come to university, to study something and to spend time with academics and other students who are all interested in similar things to you. If you work hard and engage with this it can be a fantastic experience. Learning should be enjoyable, stimulating and rewarding. Although most students now must pay for their studies, education is not something that can be bought by money alone. Education requires that you put in effort, and generally you will find that the more effort you put in, the more you get out.

The time that you spend as a student is also a great opportunity to find out about yourself. Your engagement with your subject and your degree will help you to grow as a person and to think about the things that you like and dislike and the things that you are good and not so good at. Your degree is not just preparation for your life as a worker, it is also a valuable experience in its own right.

You will also want to make sure that your degree makes a positive contribution to your career. You will have spent a lot of your time, energy, talents and money in getting your university degree, so you will want to make sure that it helps you to progress to the best possible future. In order to do this you need to understand what you are getting out of your studies so that you can think about how this might inform your career, and then clearly articulate this to potential employers.

Your degree will help to open a lot of doors to jobs that you would not have been able to get without it. To get through those doors successfully you will need to be able to:

1. recognise what you have learned and developed through your degree. This needs to include an understanding of your subject knowledge (and how it might be applied) as well as a recognition of the broader skills, abilities and aptitudes that you have developed.
2. explain to employers why what you have learned over the last three years will be able to contribute to their organisation.

This chapter will help you to recognise what your studies are offering you and to think about how they have changed you, how you can use your new knowledge and skills in the world and how you can articulate this to a potential employer.

Your subject

Let's start with your academic discipline. You might have chosen to study a topic that you enjoyed at school or one that you did particularly well in – both good reasons to decide to spend another three to four years thinking about little else! Or you may have chosen your topic because you think that it is aligned to a career outcome. Perhaps your subject offered something special that was important to you – interesting module options, well-known academics, placement or study abroad opportunities, a great nightlife etc. How about these examples:

Technical skill/knowledge/ability – *'I'm really good at maths.'*

Interest in the topic – *'I just love learning how the human brain works!'*

Aligned to a career – *'I want to go into banking so I'm studying economics.'*

Something special – *'Studying archaeology at the uni that discovered Richard III is so exciting.'*

These are all excellent reasons, and you will need these motives (alongside friends, lecturers and extra-curricular fun) to keep you going through long nights of revision and deadlines!

Connect with alumni – We mentioned graduate destinations earlier in this chapter as one way that you can learn about your university's graduates. LinkedIn is another fantastic free resource to use to connect you with alumni from your university and/or your subject. Your university might also have an in-house system for connecting with alumni for one-off events or even mentoring relationships. You might want to find out what other biologist have gone on to do, to help you explore your options. Or you might want to broaden your search to include other disciplines. If you have an idea of the field you are interested in you can search for alumni in that area. Typically, alumni are happy to provide current students and recent graduates with hints and tips about their chosen area of work. Sometimes it is easier to hear advice and guidance from someone who has been in your shoes not so long ago!

Join professional associations – Many professional associations will offer student memberships. They are keen to connect with you early in your studies, so take advantage of this and join one (or maybe two) that are relevant and meaningful for you. They often offer events, resources and connections to their membership. This is also an excellent way to demonstrate your passion and insight into an area of work – so add your new membership to your CV and LinkedIn profile!

You can also join related professional groups on LinkedIn. If you are keen to learn about the latest trends in actuarial work, then request to join one of the many actuary-related groups on LinkedIn.

CASE STUDY

Ahmed wasn't enjoying his law degree. He happened to fall in with a crowd of students who were studying accounting and went along to a Chartered Institute for Management Accountants (CIMA) event with a few of them. By the end of the session he had signed up to a student account with the professional association. He learned more about being a management accountant and attended further events, including an insight day at a firm in London.

Suddenly Ahmed found himself excited at the prospect of a career in management and this gave him the motivation to complete his degree and achieve a 2:1. The fact that he could demonstrate a good awareness of the profession through his extra-curricular interests helped him in applications and interviews, and doing research about potential employers was easy!

Would you like to ... be a management accountant?

Management accountants are responsible for preparing and analysing key financial information in an organisation to ensure that stakeholders can make informed decisions about the future of the company. They play a key role in a company's financial planning, systems and strategy.

Management accountants tend to start on a salary around £28,000. Following successful completion of professional qualifications this can rise quickly to £32,000 and above. Senior roles can earn £40,000 to upwards of £120,000. Management accountants' qualifications are usually recognised internationally, which means that they can work in different companies and opportunities around the globe. If you are looking for a role that allows you to earn well and travel, this might be for you. However, women tend to earn 24% less than men in this sector, so prepare to break that glass ceiling!

For more information on being a management accountant see Prospects, Job Profile: Chartered Management Accountant, available from Prospects (www.prospects.ac.uk/job-profiles/chartered-management-accountant). Alternatively, visit the CIMA website (www.cimaglobal.com).

TIP: GET A MENTOR!

If you are ready to explore an area of work, then consider approaching an alumnus for insights. Alumni mentoring is often something that your university will facilitate. You are likely to feel comfortable asking questions to a recent graduate and they can advise you on some of the highs and lows (and recruitment practices) in their job.

Use existing sources of support

Your university will already have numerous support services in place to help you make the most of your degree. Part of good career management is recognising these sources of support and making use of them!

Here is a list of common support services and some examples as to why you might use them.

Personal tutor	Your personal tutor is a good person to speak to about concerns or interests that you may have related to your studies. They are usually one of the academics who will write a reference for you, so it's a good idea to get to know them a bit during your degree.
Office hours	Academics will often have set times each week when they plan to meet with any students studying their course. You should make use of this time to ask relevant questions about the material.
Learning support/ development	Not sure how to structure your essay? Unsure about references or plagiarism? Struggling with effective revision techniques? Use your learning development service to make sure you are making effective use of your time and to hone your academic techniques.
Academic lecturers	Your academic lecturers are also people – people who are networked across their area of specialism and have experience in their chosen field. They may have contacts that could be of use to you. Your module leader in criminology may be doing research with the police or running a project with a local organisation. Could your lecturer assist you in contacting them to seek relevant work experience?
Students' Union	Your Students' Union will advocate on your behalf and will want to help you to enjoy university and your studies. You may wish to represent your course or create a subject-related society. This will help to expand your networks and expose you to other people with similar interests.
Careers service	Your careers service will certainly want to help you make links between your subject and your potential career. In fact, once you start listening, you might notice that they are trying to get your attention quite a lot of the time! They can help you consider the skills that you have developed and how you might address any gaps in the near future. Most careers services are still interested in helping you after you graduate, so you can still contact them long after the rented cap and gown have been returned!

Should I carry on with my subject?

One of the things you should be doing throughout your degree is thinking about whether you want to study your subject longer or maybe even make it your life's work. You may love geology and want to do little else all day, or by the end of your degree you may feel that you have seen all the rocks that you can handle.

If you think that further study is an option for you there are several things that you can be doing to explore that.

- Talk to current postgraduate and PhD students in your subject area. How did they make the decision to carry on with their subject? What do they enjoy/find difficult?
- Meet with your personal tutor to discuss further study options and recommendations.
- Research programmes of study and funding options. You can start with your own institution and then widen the net. Your personal tutor and postgraduate contacts will have some ideas to share about where you might continue your studies.
- Make the most of your dissertation or project work. Most degree programmes will include an opportunity for you to complete a large project or piece of research, typically (but not always) called your dissertation. This will normally take place in your final year. It might be at this stage in your studies that you come to realise you would like to continue being a student for a bit longer! Use your project work to explore this. Do you enjoy working independently? Are you good at it? To what extent have you developed critical thinking and research skills? Have your discovered a specialism or topic in your subject that excites you?
- Do your research – is further study in your subject going to make you more employable? Use your contacts above and your university careers service to find out where postgraduate study in your subject can lead. The website www.prospects.ac.uk offers information about postgraduate study, as do other sites such as Find a Masters (www.findamasters.com) or Find a PhD (www.findaphd.com).

You can make applications for further study and graduate jobs at the same time if you are still unsure about your preferred route. However, don't let postgraduate study become the default option. It can seem easier to just carry on being a student for one more year rather than face the 'real world'. A good test is for you to imagine you have been offered a graduate role <u>and</u> a place on a postgraduate programme of your choice. Which would you choose? If you really want the graduate role then you should work harder and concentrate your efforts on achieving that dream.

We talk more about further study in Chapter 6.

Your degree and graduate employers

In recent years there has been a lot of discussion in the news and in the higher education sector as a whole about the value of a degree. That is a big topic that deserves a chapter or even a book all on its own. But we should look at what our main consumers of graduates think. What value do graduate employers place on a university education?

Do employers care what I have studied?

Sometimes a degree subject is integral to a particular career path. Doctors need to study medicine, a software engineer will need a background in computer science and/or maths and a lawyer will have completed law school (although not necessarily as their undergraduate degree). But a great many job roles do not require you to have completed a degree in a particular subject. Business development managers, accountants, bankers, teachers, marketing and project officers – these are all examples of roles that do not require a particular academic subject.

You might then ask, what is the point of completing a degree? If an employer is happy to recruit a history student or a maths student for a role in audit and risk, then why complete a degree at all? The answer is that your degree is a bit like a driving licence. Completing it indicates that you are competent in many different skills and abilities. Employers value the core and common attributes that a graduate attains. You will have demonstrated an ability to think critically, write and communicate effectively, engage in evidence-based research, present your work to others, argue your case convincingly, retain information and work independently – in addition to a whole host of subject-specific skills that come with your chosen degree.

The other important aspect that a degree shows is your appetite for knowledge and learning new things. Employers want people who can grow and learn along with their business, the sector and the world. Your learning doesn't end at your last exam. You will be asked to apply those skills that made you successful as a student to your new role as a successful employee.

So, while what you study is not always of the utmost importance, rest assured that your degree does hold an enormous amount of value for your future prospects. Put simply, with a 'good' degree in any subject you can apply for a whole host of graduate-level jobs. Without a degree you are not going to get far in any graduate recruitment process.

CASE STUDY

Susan studied for a degree in Finance and Accounting. She was quite sure of her career path from very early on in her studies. She wanted to work as an accountant for a large, multinational company – somewhere fun and exciting that would recognise and reward her for the effort she had put into her degree subject. She applied to about a dozen well-known organisations, quietly confident that her 2:1 and related degree subject would be a winning combination. She didn't worry too much about the numerical testing – after all, her degree was full of maths! The applications were easy to complete; with a degree in Finance and Accounting Susan didn't need to dwell long on the questions and it was pretty obvious she had the skills and interest in accountancy! Weeks later Susan had not been successful beyond the second stage of any of her applications. What was going on?!

…

Stuart studied for a degree in History. It was a subject he had enjoyed at school and he was glad to have been able to specialise in the medieval period during his final year. When it came to thinking about work and careers Stuart felt he was ready to get out into the 'real world' and start earning in a graduate-level job. He did some research into different graduate roles and decided that working in accountancy would really suit him. It offered flexibility, a good salary and the chance to keep on learning with a professional qualification.

Stuart knew that he would need to be able to communicate both why he wanted to move into this profession and what skills he had developed that matched those needed in the role. He worked hard to tell this story through his applications. He spent time practising numerical testing and got his applications checked by friends for errors. In the end Stuart applied to just four well-known companies. The applications were time consuming but it was worth it, as he received an invitation to interview with two of the organisations!

The magic number: 2:1

Employers often talk about a 'good' degree. This normally refers to the level you have been awarded at the end of your degree. It could be a first, a 2:1, a 2:2, a third or a pass. It isn't always clear what constitutes a particular grade. In general the following should give you some kind of guide.

First (1)
- You will have produced consistently high-quality work which shows a sophisticated engagement with the key concepts of your degree and an ability to produce creative, well-researched and accurate assignments.

Upper second (2:1)
- You will have produced consistent work which demonstrates that you understand your subject and are able to produce assignments which are generally well researched and accurate.

Lower second (2:2)
- You will have produced adequate work which demonstrates that you understand your subject. Your work may lack creativity, accuracy or consistency.

Third
- You will have produced work which demonstrates an engagement with your subject, but which lacks theoretical sophistication and which may lack creativity, accuracy or consistency.

Pass
- You will have produced work which shows a basic level of understanding of your subject. You may have failed some modules.

Fail
- You have failed to meet the demands of the degree. It cannot be verified that you understand your subject at the degree level.

The exact criteria that are used for each of these possible outcomes will vary by university and by course. All courses should publish a module handbook that makes this clear. If you find that you are not getting the level of results that you want as you go through your course you might want to talk to one of your lecturers or your personal tutor about this and get them to explain what you could do to improve.

Graduate recruiters have a big job on their hands to sift through a large number of applications. This is one of the reasons why they ask for your degree outcome at the beginning of the process, as it can be an easy way to reduce the number of applications they have to look at. Often they will be looking for students who are 'on track' to achieve a 2:1 or above.

CASE STUDY

Versha studied a degree in Biology, a subject she loved and excelled in at secondary school. It turned out biology at university was quite a bit more difficult than she expected. She worked hard (though not always as hard as she could have done, she admits now!) and managed to achieve a 2:2.

One thing that took her mind off her studies at times was the fun she was having with the students' charity society RAG. Versha was president of the society in her final year and coordinated a number of unusual events that raised a record level of funds for local charities.

Drawing on the experience and transferable skills that she had gained in her many hours of volunteering, Versha applied to work in a national charity. It normally looked for students with a 2:1 and above but Versha's application shone and she was pleased to accept a graduate role with it in marketing. Her love of biology continues and she hopes to work for a science-related charity in the coming years. For now she is happy doing a job that she enjoys and she is thankful that her extra-curricular fun at university gave her the chance to discover her inner marketing genius!

Would you like to ... work in marketing?

People who work in marketing can work in almost any sector or type of organisation. Private sector companies require marketing departments, as do charities and your local council. Depending on the type of marketing role you are in you might be involved in planning events, advertising, copy writing, social media, product development, research and more. People who work in marketing usually enjoy working with others and have good interpersonal and organisational skills.

Salaries for marketing professionals can vary as much as the roles that they occupy and the organisations for whom they work. Entry-level roles will often start around the £20,000 mark. More senior roles can offer £40,000 and above, with marketing director roles in the private sector often commanding salaries in the £80,000-plus range.

For more information on jobs in marketing see the Prospects website (www.prospects.ac.uk/job-profiles/marketing-executive). Alternatively, visit Monster's website (www.monster.co.uk/career-advice/article/what-are-the-common-marketing-career-paths) for information about different marketing career paths.

Do employers care *where* I have studied?

It is true that some employers have a long-standing routine of recruiting from particular universities. They have always found enough suitable candidates from these campuses, so why should they spread their resources beyond them? However, increasingly, employers are wanting to recruit from a wider group of universities. With the use of online recruitment techniques such as tests and video interviews, there is little cost in spreading their recruitment around the country. Some employers have even begun omitting the name of the university that you studied at from their applications to help to ensure that they avoid any bias towards (or against) particular universities. So, where you have studied seems to be losing importance ...

One useful thing to explore is whether your university, your department or any of the academics who are teaching you have good links with any companies. You can't change the university that you are studying at, but you can find employers who think positively about it.

TIP: FOLLOW YOUR INTERESTS

It is usually a good idea to choose a degree that interests you. Once you are at university this also applies to any module options that you have. Doing well in your degree counts for a lot and you are more likely to do well when you are engaged with your subject. Of course there are exceptions where working hard at a difficult course or module will open up a particular opportunity. But, in general, focus on doing well!

What do people do with a degree in _____?

It can be useful to look at what other graduates have gone on to do with your degree. There are a number of different sources for this.

Prospects (www.prospects.ac.uk) is a good resource for general information about work related to particular degrees. However, as we've said above, many recruiters will take new graduates on from a very wide range of disciplines, so don't be boxed into the lists of typical career paths.

Destinations of Leavers of Higher Education (DLHE) statistics will give you some insight into employment statistics, types of jobs and the salaries of graduates from your own institution and degree. Google graduate destinations for your university and subject or have a look at the Unistats website (http://unistats.direct.gov.uk).

Linkedin (www.linkedin.com) gives you the chance to research graduates and investigate their career paths by reading their CVs online. You can search by university or by the name of the organisation that someone works for.

Researching a company website will very often reveal graduate profiles. These are designed as a marketing tool for new recruits (so bear that in mind!) and they will give you an idea of the degree subjects from which the company recruits.

We've mentioned earlier in this chapter that for many careers it won't matter which subject you have studied – it will be your experience, networks, motives and other attributes that will help you to get the job you want. This also applies if you have studied a particular subject with a related career path in mind. To help make the most of whatever subject you have studied, we should take a comprehensive look at your learning experience at university.

What have I *really* learned in my degree?

You will have learned a great deal about your chosen subject(s). Some of this might be facts and knowledge (eg.. the reproductive cycle of a fruit fly or the impact of the Industrial Revolution on women's rights) and some of it might be technical skills (laboratory procedures or using Bloomberg to view financial data).

ACTIVITY 2.2

Identifying your knowledge and skills

Make a list of the subject-specific knowledge and skills that you have learned in your degree. Circle any that you think an employer might be interested in. Now cross out any of those things that you would not want to do in the future. This short exercise will help you to reflect on what kinds of jobs might suit you, and perhaps more importantly, those that would not!

Employers will be interested in the facts, knowledge and technical skills you have acquired. But they will also be very interested in your capacity to learn and in what *transferable skills* you can bring with you to their organisation.

Transferable or employability skills, as they are also known, are skills and attributes that you develop in one arena (serving customers at a local fast-food restaurant or working with a group of peers on a presentation, for example) and that you can then apply in another setting (dealing with clients in your online sales business or organising a promotional event with your marketing team). You can transfer these skills from one type of activity and use them in another. Employers look for evidence of transferable skills as part of their recruitment practices and it is your responsibility to make sure that they can find that evidence in the form of effective examples.

Your degree will be structured in such a way as to offer you opportunities to develop transferable skills. Some of this will be quite obvious – for example, there may be a list of skills that you are expected to develop as part of the learning outcomes of a module. Others will be more subtle – perhaps developed through classroom activities or assessments.

A good way of identifying transferable skills in your discipline is to simply look at a list and identify your own examples. Below is a comprehensive list of transferable skills. We've provided some sample definitions and examples to illustrate what we mean by a particular skill and how it might be developed as part of your degree. Of course you can also develop these skills in other areas of your life and experience. We've also included examples of careers in which these skills might be of particular value.

When looking at this list consider some of the types of work that you have completed in your degree. There may be online or class tests, lectures, exams, project work, essays, tutorials, presentations and group projects. Each of these activities will require you to exercise some of the skills listed in the table below. For example, an independent piece of work such as a dissertation requires digital literacy, independent thinking, initiative and self-direction, multi-tasking, research skills, self-management, time management and writing skills.

Transferable skills – a comprehensive list!

Transferable skill	I developed this ...	Useful in a career as a ...
Aspiration		
Autonomy		
Career management		
Communication skills		
Creativity		
Critical thinking skills The ability to analyse and evaluate information to come to a rational decision or judgement. Being able to recognise the value of different sources of data.	*I analysed three research articles as part of the background research for my dissertation. I had to consider different sources of information and decide which were the most reliable and appropriate. I analysed the different perspectives and used the sources to help inform my viewpoint.*	*Editor, Researcher, Auditor*

Customer awareness		
Digital literacy		
Efficiency		
Emotional intelligence		
Enterprise and entrepreneurship		
Ethics		
Flexibility and adaptability		
Giving and receiving feedback		
Independent thinking		
Initiative and self-direction		
Interpersonal skills The ability to listen to and communicate with others effectively. An awareness of others' perspectives and an understanding of how to interact with other people.	*I worked with others on a group project. It was difficult as not all members brought the same level of enthusiasm, effort and commitment. I ensured that we met regularly and continued to communicate where we were with the project with the whole team. We set review dates and encouraged each other to complete the necessary work. Although it was frustrating at times I enjoyed working with our team members and recognised that we each brought different strengths to the table.*	*Human Resources Officer, Teacher, Project Manager, Business Consultant*
Language skills		
Multi-tasking		
Numeracy		
Opportunity awareness The ability to recognise a chance to learn something new, meet new people and/or gain new skills. Being able to see beyond an immediate activity to what it has the capacity to lead to.	*My module leader asked for volunteers to work on her research project. Although the work itself was boring I learned a lot about the processes involved in experiment design, project management and research. I'm now getting paid on a part-time basis while I finish my degree (and she's been a lot of help with my dissertation!)*	*Recruitment Advisor, Investment Banker, Events Coordinator*

Positive attitude		
Presentation skills		
Problem-solving		
Professional knowledge		
Research skills		
Resilience		
Self-management		
Social intelligence		
Teamworking		
Time management The ability to prioritise activities according to their importance and value within a particular context. Being able to anticipate potential issues and make adjustments as required to ensure work is delivered in the required time frame.	*I had three significant pieces of coursework due on the same day in my final year. I looked ahead and prioritised my work to get them all done on time and to an excellent standard. I ensured I had the resources needed in good time and set a schedule to track my progress. I allowed time to review my work before submission.*	*Chef, Logistics Planner, Marketing Manager*
Willingness (and capability) to learn		
Work ethic		
Writing skills		

Evidencing your subject skills

In an ideal world you would be able to provide an example for each of the transferable skills above through your work experience, achievements and academic studies. But you don't need to complete the entire table – you aren't supergirl after all!

Instead take time to identify the skills that are seen as particularly important in a job that is of interest to you. Are you able to provide effective examples of these transferable skills? How will you talk about this to an employer?

What have you been most interested in or enjoyed the most? What does that tell you about your career plans?

IN A NUTSHELL

- Research possible outcomes from your subject. There are likely to be many!
- Practise telling your story – employers want to know why you studied your subject, what skills you have learned and how that relates to their needs.
- Your degree is about more than the subject – spend time listing the types of skills that you have developed and how you might use your degree to evidence them.
- Don't assume that your degree subject will automatically mean you fit into a particular industry or role.
- Use all available sources of support to help you do well in your degree and to assist you in your decisions about jobs.
- Consider further study, but do your research!
- Get connected to your subject or area of interest through alumni, professional associations, student groups and your department.

3 ARE YOU EXPERIENCED?

Work experience is something that is talked about a lot by employers and candidates. Candidates are often saying they need it and employers are often saying that they need candidates with lots of it. We have the classic catch 22 – how do you get work experience without any work experience in the first place?!

There is no doubt that it is very important for university students to get work experience alongside their degree for lots of different reasons. Happily, university students are actually in a fantastic position to obtain excellent work experience. In fact you may never have so many different opportunities on your doorstep as you do right now.

This chapter will help you to:

■ understand why work experience is important

■ recognise the experience you already have

■ identify new and different opportunities

■ make the most of any experience you have.

Introduction

Throughout this chapter we will talk about 'work experience' but you will notice that sometimes the experience we are talking about does not include paid work. This is because there are so many different ways that you can access work experience. Under the 'Work Experience' section on your CV you might list paid work, volunteering, placements (paid and unpaid), shadowing, competitions, projects and positions of responsibility. The word 'work' has a much broader meaning than you might think. We can talk about 'voluntary work', 'part-time work', 'working hard on your course' and even 'housework'. Work doesn't have to be paid and it definitely doesn't just have to relate to a graduate job, so we'd encourage you to think broadly about your work experience. Whatever work experience you have, whether it is your Easter break spent saving turtles in Cuba or your part-time job in the dry cleaners, you will find that it will be helpful in enabling employers to see how useful you could be to them.

Why is work experience so important?

1. Work experience will help you learn.

Work experience is a very important way that we learn and grow. Think about your favourite hobby or sport. Think about the time you have spent doing it, practising it, getting better and discovering new ways to enjoy it. That learning and development happens as a result of the experiences you have had.

You might hear lecturers or career professionals talk about a learning theory called experiential learning or Kolb's Learning Cycle.[ii] Kolb's Learning Cycle is a model of learning that focuses on how individuals learn from experiences.

The cycle divides learning into four distinct stages: concrete experience (when we do things); reflection and observation (when we think about how an experience went); abstraction and conceptualisation (when we think about what this experience means and consider how it might change the way that we see the world or behave in the future); and active experimentation (when we apply some of the new ideas to our experience).

Concrete experience

'I really enjoy playing basketball for my league.'

Reflection and observation

'Well I didn't score any points at today's game but I did manage to guard well.'

Active experimentation

'I'm trying out my new technique at practice today. Hope to score more baskets at tomorrow's game!'

Abstract conceptualisation

'After the game our coach gave me some tips about my layup technique and using visualisation.'

You can see that in this model of learning the experiences that we have play a central role. Without the experience the other stages don't make sense. Experience is everything!

Your work experience gives you the opportunity to learn, grow and develop in a number of different ways. You will learn more about yourself, what you enjoy and what you are good at. This is so important to being able to make good decisions about your career that we devoted almost an entire chapter to it (Chapter 1, I just don't know what to do with myself). Experimenting with different types of experiences will help you to get to know more about your likes, dislikes, values, priorities and strengths. You will also learn more about different types of work. Something that you thought would be very interesting might turn out to be deathly dull on a day-to-day basis – and vice versa.

2. **Work experience is a safe place to experiment.**

You can use your time spent volunteering or working in part-time roles and summer jobs as a chance to try new things and to road-test a career option. Just because you are helping out at an after-school club doesn't mean that you have to commit to a career as a teacher. If something doesn't feel quite right, have a think about what that might mean. Is it the circumstances, your confidence, your skills or something more central to your personality that means this particular experience (career) is not for you? Learning what doesn't appeal is often as helpful as learning what does!

Volunteering is a particularly good option for road-testing a career. Volunteers are often given a lot of responsibility and opportunities for training and events that otherwise might not be supported.

3. **Work experience is evidence of your passion.**

Having work experience can help to show that you are genuinely interested in that area of work. You will be able to demonstrate that you have given your options some thought and that you are passionate about your chosen career path.

4. **Work experience can help to get you connected.**

While you might not be able to volunteer for the CEO of a successful charity, you might find that volunteering at one of their shops will help to you get one step closer to their sphere of influence. You can befriend senior members of the team, read the staff newsletter to find out about new campaigns and attend training events that could put you next to someone who knows the head honcho in recruitment!

5. **Work experience makes you more successful in applications and interviews.**

Applicants with work experience outperform those with no work experience. This is likely to be for all of the reasons we have highlighted above. Why wouldn't an employer prefer a candidate who knows themselves well, knows something about the career they are entering, has experimented in that arena and can demonstrate their passion for the sector? But it is worth mentioning that having work experience, of any kind, simply makes it easier to complete the application and interview stages of recruitment. Employers will ask questions about your experience, knowledge and interest in the job. They are looking for clear examples and evidence of this.

CASE STUDY

Sean worked in a fast-food restaurant before he joined university. He liked serving customers and enjoyed the fast pace, flexibility and pay. When he went to university one of his priorities was to find part-time work so that he would have money for fun non-essentials. He applied for a weekend sales job at a large furniture store. They seemed pleased that he was confident when interacting with customers. Sean ended up working at the shop throughout his three years at university, eventually becoming a team leader with additional responsibilities.

He didn't start to consider his long-term career options until the middle of his final year. He thought about what he had learned about himself and about work to date. He knew that he liked solving problems for his customers, he enjoyed leading others in the team and he preferred busy chaotic days to quieter days with fewer customers.

He researched some graduate career options and went to see his university careers service for some advice. The job descriptions for business consultant matched a lot of Sean's likes and strengths. It wasn't a job he'd ever heard of, but the more he learned about it the more it sounded like the kind of thing he could relate to and enjoy. He also found it easier to write applications for these roles. When it came to interview he was able to talk with confidence about his understanding of good customer service and he could see that the panel were impressed with the reference his employer at the furniture store had provided.

In the end it was Sean's work experience that helped him to learn and develop his skills. He found a career path that he'd not yet considered by looking at what he knew about himself. All of this gave him the edge in applications and interviews.

We've established that work experience is important for a number of different reasons. Now let's turn our attention to the experience you already have and how you might go about getting more.

I don't have any experience

Not everyone has spent their summer working in an office or volunteering to save the whales. And of course it is perfectly reasonable for a younger person to struggle to fill the 'Work Experience' section of their CV. So what do you do if you don't feel you have any experience?

The first thing to do is to double check that this is really the case. Remember that work experience includes a lot of things that you might not class as 'work'. It also includes work that may not appear to be directly relevant to the career you are seeking. Your time spent working in the Fish and Chip Palace every Friday night does count and should be included on your CV. So does captaining the university football team, volunteering to help children to read, acting as treasurer of the Curry Society and a whole host of other activities.

Are you confident you have included everything?

CASE STUDY

Ash spent many evenings after school helping out in the family's convenience store. She could be doing anything from serving customers to stacking shelves or ordering in new stock. It became just part of who she was. Ash didn't really class this as work because she wasn't getting paid in the traditional sense, she'd never interviewed for the job and there wasn't even a job title.

When Ash turned her attention to her CV she found it difficult to complete the 'Work Experience' section. Apart from the shop work, some babysitting and a one-week placement that she did at school she didn't have a lot to add.

Ash went to her careers advisor for help and he helped her to see that her years of working in her family shop had given her a wealth of knowledge and skills about running a business. He helped Ash to write a skills-based CV that highlighted all the examples of her abilities really well. She was able to emphasise her skills, and her work experience section looked much more respectable.

This in turn gave Ash a good reference point for applications and interviews. She had a better understanding of the value of her experience and could talk about it with more confidence in her applications and interviews. Re-thinking and re-framing her experience made a big difference. Ash feels that this had a big part to play in her successful application for a summer internship position with a well-known retailer. She is now entering a graduate management trainee programme with the same company.

Would you like to ... work in retail management?

There are several graduate schemes with large retail companies. Some may focus on particular business functions, such as management, buying, merchandising or logistics, whereas others are more overarching in their approach.

You don't have to have a degree to go into retail management but it is an advantage and will mean that you can enter the company in a management role rather than working your way up from sales clerk. Most companies will recruit from any discipline but they might look more favourably on business or management degrees.

Employers in retail management look for candidates with a breadth of skills. The role is likely to be quite varied and this is reflected in the job outlines. Expect to be able to demonstrate effective skills in communication, influencing people, leadership, problem-solving and organisation.

On a graduate programme you can expect a competitive starting salary of £20,000–£25,000 and above. Sometimes there will be benefits such bonus schemes or a company car.

Target Jobs (https://targetjobs.co.uk/career-sectors/retail-buying-and-merchandising) offers a good site for learning more about applying for jobs in this sector.

Another way to look at work experience is to think about the skills that you have developed. This might help you to newly recognise and value things that you have done – see Activity 3.1 on the following page.

If you have done this and you still feel that you are lacking experience, then the thought of writing a CV can be daunting. But there are ways around this. (1) You can write a skills-focused CV to make up for any deficits in your 'Work Experience' section. (2) Keep your CV to one page to minimise the emphasis on the experience section until you have more to include there. You will find more information on this in Chapter 7, where we focus on applications for work.

Recognising your skills

What are three or four skills that you know are important in a sector or job that interests you? List these in the table below. An example might be a journalist – with communication, independence and an ability to cope with tight deadlines.

Next think about all the ways in which you might finish the statement 'I did this when I …'

What experiences do you already have that you might use to demonstrate that you have developed that particular skill or ability?

After you have completed the table ask a friend or family member to add their thoughts. They may have a different view from you and may recall different aspects of your work experiences.

Skill/ability	I did this when I ...	My friend/family member says ...
Communication	Worked part time in cafe (but I was mostly in the back prepping the food and cleaning up)	I remember you also helped to organise their big external events. You had to order the right amounts of food and make sure it was all prepped in time. Remember when there was that big 50th birthday party and you became the main point of contact for the whole thing? It sounded really difficult and you dealt with their never-ending phone calls and emails so well!

Finding new things to add to your experience

Now that we have done our best to exhaust your existing work experience let's look at how we can find you some new work experience.

Part-time paid work

Whether it is in the summer, after lectures or at weekends, part-time paid work is often the preferred choice for students at university. There can be a sense that this is more valuable to your career development than other, non-paid experiences.

Remember to consider your studies when choosing work. It won't help to get a part-time job 20 hours per week if it means that you fail some of your modules or can't attend some lectures! Most universities provide guidelines as to how many hours of work per week you can do during term time. It is advisable to stay within these recommendations. International students have quite strict regulations on the number of hours of work they can do. Consult your international student advisor for more information.

Volunteering

Volunteering is an excellent option. You can work in a field that really interests you, get to know the sector and increase your contacts. Your Students' Union or careers service will often have a dedicated staff member or student who acts as a main point of contact for volunteering opportunities in the local community. Most large towns have a volunteering organisation as well. Failing that, you can try the website www.do-it.org, which allows you to search by the type of role you want and your postcode. Have a go and you will be amazed at what you might find on your doorstep.

Remember that volunteering carries with it a burden of responsibility. Don't take on something new just to boost your CV. Find something that you think you will be interested in, where you can learn something new and that you will enjoy. Invest time in your volunteering and you will be rewarded.

It can take time to get your volunteering placement up and running. Sometimes there are safety checks such as DBS (Disclosure and Barring Service) that need to be completed, or mandatory training as part of an induction. Plan your volunteering to fit in with your medium-term plans (the next year or so). Both you and the organisation will benefit from sustained engagement.

Would you like to be ... a volunteer coordinator?

Managing volunteers can be a rewarding and fun career, and with a variety of responsibilities. You might be expected to be the main point of contact and manager of a project and to recruit, train and support your volunteers throughout their involvement. You would need to be aware of health and safety policies and legislation relating to volunteers and your area of work.

Some volunteer coordinators start their roles as unpaid volunteers themselves. The salary, as you might expect in the charity sector, is not particularly high, with starting salaries in the £15,000–£20,000 range. More experienced, senior volunteer coordinators earn more, but it would be unusual for a volunteer coordinator to earn upwards of £35,000. Higher earners are likely to be working on high-profile campaigns.

A role such as this can rely on external funding such as government initiatives or charity fundraising. This can mean that there is some level of job insecurity.

The Association of Volunteer Managers (https://volunteermanagers.org.uk) is a professional association that offers support, training, policy and research for those working in the role.

When looking for work in this area you can look at Charity Job (www. charityjob.co.uk), but you might also find that getting connected to your local or regional volunteering centre will help to keep you informed of new projects and roles.

Students' Union/halls/sports

There are a surprising amount and variety of activities going on in most Students' Unions. Alongside the football club you are likely to find an environmental campaign group, a knitting club, a historical re-enactment group, language-swapping schemes and even a quidditch squad. Even better, if you don't find a club that interests you, then this is the perfect time to set up your own. Students' Unions are well equipped to help you get a club off the ground.

All of these clubs will have meetings, trips and activities to plan and attend. Some will obtain sponsorship or will have membership fees to manage. All of this takes work from the core team members. With all the different types of activities going on there is enough opportunity for work experience for practically every student on campus.

You might also want to consider whether you would like to take on an elected role in the Students' Union. There are a wide range of roles that take up very different amounts of time. A seat on the union council might require you to attend a meeting every couple of weeks, while officer roles (e.g. Women's Officer, Environmental Officer) may require a bit more dedication. There is also usually a handful of leadership roles (including president!). What better work experience could you ask for than a year of running a business? Most of today's politicians (especially those in the Labour party) got their start in student politics. So get your election promises in order and start campaigning!

Competitions

Another way to develop skills and build your experience is to join in one of the many competitions aimed at undergraduates and recent graduates. Employers have discovered that competitions are an effective way of marketing their companies to potential new recruits – and an even better way of spotting talented candidates. These types of competitions are often team-based projects such as the Universities Business Challenge (www.ubcworldwide. com) or WildHeart's Micro-Tyco (http://wildheartsgroup.com/micro-tyco), to name just two. You will also find competitions that are targeted at students who are studying your subject area, such as marketing and design competitions, competitions focusing on sustainable energy solutions and academic competitions similar to television's University Challenge. Student Competitions. Com (www.studentcompetitions.com) offers a helpful database of these competitions.

Shadowing opportunities

There is a lot to be said for gaining experience in the industry that you are interested in working in. Unfortunately this is often difficult to find. But you will find it much easier to get a short, unpaid work shadowing opportunity.

A shadowing placement lasts normally one to two weeks and is generally unpaid. You would be expected to watch and learn by following a member or members of staff throughout the working day. Shadowing opportunities can be limited, as, unlike a longer, paid placement, they do not usually allow you to get stuck into projects and apply your skills in the workplace. But they do offer you the chance to learn a lot about a job role and industry. And it can mean that you can add a well-respected company name to your CV.

Use all the connections you may have – friends, family, LinkedIn groups, academics, your careers service – to help you identify and approach potential contacts. The key to being successful is to be clear about what you think you would be able to contribute in a short period and to be professional and courteous in your approaches.

A lot of companies will find the idea of a short unpaid placement unusual and may point you towards their placement and internships schemes instead. You can apply for those and carry on your search for a short-term shadowing opportunity elsewhere.

Working at your university or department

Universities employ hundreds, if not thousands, of part-time staff across an academic year. Some of these people will be working in your own department/school in administrative roles or as research project assistants. Find out where the jobs board for your university can be found – is there an organisation that you need to register with in order to receive emails about jobs?

You can also approach some of your favourite academics and let them know that you have time available to them and an interest in their research. They may have data analysis, data inputting or experiment administration work and would love some help!

Side projects

You might have an idea of your own for a project that you would like to work on in your spare time. It could be a business idea that you want to develop, a piece of research that you want to explore or perhaps a technology that you want to experiment with. If you genuinely have the time and resources to devote to something like this, then there is often a lot to be gained from giving it a go. You might want to bring others in on your idea and/or look for support from the entrepreneurship arm of your careers service.

Depending on the application of your 'side project' and what you have learned from the experience, you may want to bring this to the attention of a potential recruiter by mentioning it on your CV or in an application. It can be the kind of thing that makes you stand out in the recruitment process as someone with creativity, drive and resilience.

Extended work experience

Your three-year degree will go by so quickly. So why not extend it by a year? Most universities offer you the opportunity to undertake a placement year (also known as a year in industry or a 'sandwich degree') as part of your degree. This is a year in which you will work in a university-approved setting. These placements are paid. Even if your university does not offer an official year in industry programme it is possible for you to pause your studies for one year to take up a placement year with a company. Make sure that you get advice about funding, visas and pausing your studies. The benefits of taking a year out to work in industry are well recognised. Students who complete a placement year tend to be in graduate-level work within a few months after graduation.[iii]

Another way to lengthen your time as a student and to gain experience is to study abroad for a year or term. Again, many universities offer this as an option, so get some advice about what your university has to offer. In addition to being lots of fun there are many employability-related benefits to studying abroad. You can demonstrate your resilience, tenacity, language-learning skills, cultural awareness, global mindset and other key skills.

Employers are always pleased to see that students have taken up these opportunities. Your additional year of study will give you a bit more time to explore and grow. Ultimately this experience will help you to make those important decisions about your next steps in terms of career and life.

Internships (summer and graduate)

Summer internships are another excellent way to get industry-related experience. These are often limited to penultimate year students, as employers use them as a recruitment tool for their graduate-level positions. Successful completion of a summer internship will often mean that you can skip some of the usual recruitment stages – you might go straight to the interview or assessment day! Summer internships are competitive and the recruitment for them can start as early as August for the following summer.

Graduate internships are less numerous (most graduate opportunities are simply called 'jobs' and don't have short-term contracts applied to them). Where they do exist they will normally last anywhere from three to nine months and they will be paid. A graduate internship may have a slightly lower starting salary, but it will very often open the door to a better role at the end of the scheme.

To give you the best chance of success, research your chosen scheme and follow our advice about applications and assessment centres in Chapter 7.

Unpaid internships

You might be wondering if you would have more luck getting an unpaid internship. While it does seem as if offering your time and talent for free would be an offer that most employers wouldn't refuse, in fact you won't find many companies actively offering an unpaid internship. There are a couple of reasons for this, the most important of which boils down to equality.

There has been recognition in recent years that unpaid internships are opportunities that are only really open to those who can afford them. Industries that support unpaid internships are less likely to attract candidates from a variety of social backgrounds. Who can afford to work for free for two months just to get experience? So, at the heart of the issue is fair and equal opportunity for all. Unpaid internships are actually a topic that is under discussion in the current government as it reviews employment practices as a whole, with some saying there should be a ban on unpaid internships.

There are some industries that have long-held traditions of unpaid internships. These have, in the past, included journalism, museums, media, marketing and charities, among others. Despite the concerns outlined above you may come across an unpaid internship that seems like a very good opportunity. Before you decide to take it up you should make sure that you are very clear about what you hope to gain from the experience. Gaining work experience is valuable, but will you be able to expect a paid role at the end of your internship? Will the contacts, connections and knowledge serve you well when the internship is over? Make sure that you discuss your terms with the employer. You'll want to be sure that you understand how long the internship will last, what the responsibilities will be and what expenses you can expect to be paid (travel or training costs, for example).

If you have any questions about your rights as a worker (paid or unpaid), then we recommend that you visit the government's employment rights website (www.gov.uk/employment-rights-for-interns), which clarifies workers' rights and employers' responsibilities.

Volunteering/working abroad schemes

There are a number of well-recognised schemes that offer you the chance to work or volunteer aboard. Sometimes these will pay you, though often not a great deal and not enough to entirely fund your travels. Other times there will be a fee for you to pay for the organisation to set up your progranmme. Either way, these represent great opportunities, interesting work experience and often an unusual way to see a particular country. Camp America, Frontier and Bunac are three well-known organisations who run these types of schemes. Before you choose a scheme be sure to check for recommendations and visit your careers service to find out what they already know about the organisation.

Making the most of your work experience

You have a good understanding of why employers value work experience, you've audited your own work experience to date and identified the different types of opportunities you might like to follow up in the near future. So, how can you ensure that you make the most of the work experience you have?

The first and probably most obvious thing to say is – do it well!

You want your peers, colleagues and managers to be glad that they got the chance to work with you and to welcome you back with open arms – even if you aren't interested in going back. Behave professionally and courteously. Arrive on time. Do what you say you will do. Take on extra responsibilities where possible. All of this will lead to good recommendations and references. It may even lead to other job roles in the future. Keep a record of your connections via your work experience – you may find that later on in life your manager at the tourist office is just the person to ask for a reference as flight attendant!

Put it on your CV

As soon as you begin a new role make sure that you add it to your CV and LinkedIn profile. Give a general description of your duties and responsibilities. As you develop in the role you can add to the skills section of your CV to illustrate which skills this job has particularly helped you to develop. Don't leave a job out just because you are not sure if it is relevant. You should have at least one version of your CV that includes all of your work experience. As that section grows you can pick and choose the roles that you feel most proud of, excited about or that you feel are most closely aligned to your chosen career path.

TIP: USE FRIENDS AND FAMILY!

Have a friend or family member read your CV to see what they think. Have you made the most of your experiences? Are you missing anything? Could you use different examples to better illustrate your skills and experiences?

Match potential job descriptions to your skills

It's important to know what kinds of skills you will need in your new job after graduation. There are some that are relatively common in all graduate roles, such as communication skills, teamwork, leadership and the ability to work independently. It is worth looking at a few of your favourite dream job descriptions and identifying the skills listed as requirements for those roles. Can you provide examples from your work experience to demonstrate your understanding and ability in those areas?

This will be particularly important when it comes to recruitment activities such as applications and interviews. You will be asked questions such as 'Tell us about a time when you led a team' and 'Provide an example in which you demonstrated effective communication skills'. Using the STAR technique (Situation, Task, Action, Result) to structure your answers will help to ensure that you are utilising your work experience to maximum effect. We discuss STAR in more depth in Chapter 7, 'Successful applications and interviews'.

Reflect on your work experience

Have you enjoyed your work experience? Why or why not? What have you learned? Could you imagine spending more time in that sort of industry and developing your responsibilities? These are all important sorts of questions to ask yourself.

You might have discovered some important clues about the type of work you really love, or really don't enjoy. If this is an area of work that you would like to continue to explore, then get busy doing that as soon as possible. Make your boss or favourite colleague aware that you would like to learn more. Ask if you can return to shadow someone more senior or work part-time while you are at university. Keeping your relationship with the organisation alive means that you will have someone to speak to about potential opportunities – and a great industry reference ready to support you when you make an application.

If the answer to the first question, 'Have you enjoyed your work experience?' is a resounding 'NO!' then take a moment to think about why that was the case. Was there an overbearing boss? A particularly difficult project? Or perhaps there was nothing wrong with the organisation or industry but you didn't enjoy the junior-level work. The answers to these questions are worth thinking about to make sure that you don't dismiss a career option based on one negative experience.

IN A NUTSHELL

- Work experience is an important part of how you learn about yourself – reflect on what you have learned and use it to help you make effective career decisions.
- Use work experience to experiment with different career options.
- Recognise the different types of experiences that have shaped who you are.
- Challenge yourself to find different types of opportunities.
- Make the most of your work experience by identifying your transferable skills and making use of your network.

4 IT'S NOT WHAT YOU KNOW, IT'S WHO YOU KNOW

You've probably heard that having a good network can open up opportunities for you in your career. But lots of people are scared of networking. This chapter will examine the benefits that a good network can offer you and suggest ways in which you can build your networks while you are at university.

This chapter will help you to:

- think about why networking matters and how it can help you to move your career forward

- consider some of the principles that underpin effective networking

- think about what kind of networking you can do as a student

- think about what kind of networking you should do once you start work.

Introduction

You've probably heard someone say, often in anger, 'You know, it's not what you know, it's who you know'. Generally, when people are saying this they are annoyed about some unfairness that they have experienced in the workplace. Perhaps you've heard that the boss's son has just been promoted, or that all of the senior management team went to the same exclusive public school. This kind of thing is more common than you might think, and once you start noticing it, it is easy to get (justifiably) bitter. But, while being 'well connected' can lead to some unfair practices, we all have to recognise that, at least to some extent, it is part of the way organisations work, and learn to use it to our advantage. In this chapter we're going to explain why networks are so important, and also to argue that they may not be an entirely bad thing.

Most work is highly social. This is a good thing and psychologists argue that the fact that you get to make friends and interact with people is one of the main things that keeps people coming back to work every day.[iv] Human beings are social animals and so, to some extent, building a network is just part of being human. We don't normally call it 'networking', we normally just call it 'making friends' or 'having a laugh'. However, if you are going to turn your normal friendliness into a network that is supportive of your career you probably need to think a bit more about who you talk to, why you are talking to them and how you sustain these relationships over the long term.

The fact that people want to work with people they like often means that they like to work with people they know. This is one of the reasons why we tell our friends when we see opportunities in our companies that we think would be good for them. We want to help them out, but we also want to strengthen our workplace network and make work more enjoyable. Employers are generally keen to appoint people that they know because every time they appoint a new person that they don't know they are taking a risk. There are various kinds of risks that an employer is taking when they appoint someone. These include the fact that a new team member might:

■ not have the knowledge or skills to do the job
■ be incredibly lazy or difficult to work with

- not get on with the rest of the team and upset them
- be an unpleasant individual.

Where that person is already a known quantity the risk is diminished. So, one way to think about networking is to recognise that you are often making an impression on people who might be your potential employer in the future.

CASE STUDY

Amrita is a biological sciences student who is coming towards the end of her third year at university. During her time at university she has become very interested in public attitudes towards science. She would really like to carry on working on this and investigates various career options that are about communicating science to the general public in a variety of ways.

Amrita goes to talk to her favourite lecturer, who runs the module that she took on Scientific Communication. Dr Singh directs her towards some of his contacts in the university, some pressure groups and the media. Amrita makes contact with all of these people and asks if she can come and see them and ask them some questions. About half of them reply and say that they are willing to talk to her. She uses the conversations to find out about their careers, to ask them for any other contacts that they have and to enquire about any events that she could attend or any opportunities for volunteering. Quite a few take her up on her offer and she finds herself running the reception desk at a charity event and helping to show visitors to the university around the biology labs.

After she graduates Amrita gets a job in a call centre, but keeps in touch with her science communication contacts. She continues to volunteer with them and gets to know some of the people in the field pretty well. Six months after graduation a project assistant job comes up in science communication and she applies for it. When she walks into the interview room she realises that she knows everyone on the panel ...

Would you like to ... work in science communication?

If you are interested in working in the communication of science to the general public there are probably quite a range of jobs that you could do. For example, it would be possible to argue that all science teachers in schools are engaged in this kind of activity, as are people involved in university outreach, museum education, scientific journalism, public relations and a host of other areas. What unites these jobs is a passion for science and an interest in finding ways to communicate it to a range of different non-specialist audiences.

If you are interested in getting involved in the public communication of science you will need to be able to show that you have a strong interest in science. Usually having a relevant degree will help and there is also a wide range of jobs needing to be filled by people with postgraduate-level science training. Being able to demonstrate that you have communicated science to others also will be key to finding a role. Good evidence includes writing your own blog, being involved in university science communication initiatives, volunteering in museums and contributing to publications such as the student newspaper on scientific subjects.

It is difficult to say how much you might earn in this field, as this will vary significantly depending on experience and specialism. An entry-level role would likely have an annual salary of £15,000–£20,000, rising with experience.

The Network for the Public Communication of Science and Technology (www.pcst.co) is a good place to make contacts and find out more about this field.

You can also visit the Prospects website for roles relating to science (www.prospects.ac.uk/jobs-and-work-experience/job-sectors/science-and-pharmaceuticals).

Why network?

Networking is not just a case of meeting potential employers. There is a wide range of reasons why you might want to build a network.

- **To find out what is going on.** The more people you know, the more likely you are to find out useful information about how different careers and companies work and to hear about opportunities.
- **To learn from others' career experiences.** Talking to a range of people, especially people who are at a different stage from you in their career, can give you ideas and inspiration. Why not start asking people what they were doing at your age?
- **To get support (and, just as importantly, to provide support for others).** Networks provide ways for you to give and receive support and encouragement. Networks run on this kind of reciprocity and you may find that the more you help others, the more help you see coming back your way.
- **To get better known.** Being part of a network can raise your profile and help you to build your reputation. A network is not just who you know but also who knows you. If other people know who you are and what you are good at they may spot opportunities and pass them along to you.
- **To have fun!** Ultimately, networking is just about talking to people. If you do it right, it can be fun and interesting.

How to network

Networking describes a process of making, maintaining and managing professional connections. Effective networkers are able to meet new people and keep in touch with them. They are also good at making sure that they are particularly close to the ones who are really useful to their career.

Some people are uncomfortable with networking because they feel that it is just 'using people' and that it can interfere with real friendships and relationships. However, there are three key principles that should make you feel positive about networking.

1. **Reciprocity.** Effective networkers need to give as much as they take. If all you ever hear from someone is 'Can you help me?' or 'I need a favour', it probably won't be long before you stop answering your phone to them. Effective networkers are generous and give their time and advice to others. Because they do that, people are willing to support them when they ask for help in return.
2. **Equity.** Effective networkers treat people equally and don't just talk to the most important person in the room. It is much more beneficial to be nice

to everyone, to be interested in them and to treat them with respect. The people you meet may offer a wide range of ideas and insights that might be helpful to your career. What is more, they may be future friends or colleagues. It is also always worth remembering that you never know who the person you are talking to knows. Someone may be at the bottom of the pile but might still be a regular confidant (or partner or relative) of the woman at the top.

3. **Authenticity.** Effective networkers keep it real! Of course you want to show people the best side of you, but you shouldn't pretend to be someone else. Putting on a fake accent, pretending that you are interested in golf when you aren't or telling outright lies about where you went to school or university are all VERY BAD ideas. People are amazingly good at spotting a fake and will often punish you for your attempted deception.

Being honest, generous and decent are huge benefits in effective networking. But that isn't the whole story. Effective networkers can be good guys but they also need to be well planned and clear about what they are trying to achieve. The next three principles of networking highlight this.

4. **Strategy.** Effective networkers think about who they are trying to network with and why. Just meeting lots of people and chatting with them won't help your career. If you want to be a successful lawyer why are you spending all of your time hanging out with doctors? Your time is limited, so you need to make sure that you are spending it wisely, going to the right events and following the right people online.

5. **Tenacity.** Effective networkers make sure that they maintain relationships (that is why reciprocity is so important). If you meet an employer or useful contact try to follow up the next day with an email and then keep in regular touch with them.

6. **Evaluation.** Effective networkers review their approach to networking and think about how they could do it better. You may find that you've been attending events with employers but they haven't generated any opportunities. If so, think about how you could refocus your time. Alternatively, you may find that your network is growing and growing. But knowing lots of people is no use if you don't have any time to actually talk to them. You should evaluate your network and work out who you want to spend time interacting with. As your network develops this will be more important than meeting new people.

All six of these principles of networking are important. You will need to keep them in mind, whether you are networking face to face or online.

Overcoming your fear of networking

It is all very well to set out a bunch of principles for networking, but this jumps right past the key issue.

NETWORKING IS SO EMBARRASSING!

Meeting new people is hard for everyone. But it is especially hard when you are at the beginning of your career and you seem to be taking a lot more than you can give. When you go to networking events it often seems as if everyone else knows each other and you're left sitting on the edge of the room, like the wallflower at the school disco.

You can take some comfort in knowing that everyone finds it hard to start the process of building a network. But there are some things that you can do to make it easier.

- **Start online.** It is easier to get to know someone face to face if you have already made a connection online. An increasing amount of networking happens online but, just as with face-to-face conversations, the number of contacts isn't as important as the quality of them. Three thousand Facebook friends won't help you if you can't remember who any of them are.
- **Start with the people that you know.** Networking is not just about meeting new people, it is also about keeping in touch with the people that you already know. If you have met someone once, go up to them and say 'Hi, remember me?' Once you've met them a few times they will be a proper part of your network.
- **Hunt in packs.** It can be easier to approach people if you are not alone. Why not work with a friend or course mate when you first start networking?
- **Get prepared.** When you go up to someone that you don't know it can be easy to get tongue tied. You can prepare three simple questions to get you started, e.g. (1) 'How did you get your current job?' (2) 'What advice would you offer me if I wanted to work at your company?' (3) 'What is the most common thing that gets an application rejected?' The point of these questions is as much to get you started as it is to find out the answer.

- **Talk about yourself (but not too much).** When you are meeting people it is important to provide them with enough information about you to form an impression. So tell them what you are studying, what you like about it and what you are thinking of doing next. Be positive and upbeat but don't go on too long. Try to ask them a question about themselves and their organisation for every piece of information that you give.
- **Remember that they are just people.** The people you are networking with are people first and network contacts second. They will have interests and dreams about things other than work. Sometimes talking about a shared interest can be a powerful way to make a contact. Most of the graduate recruiters who visit universities are fairly young. For many it will be only a few years since they sat where you sat. Why not ask them where they studied and why they chose the career path that they have followed?

Building your network

A network is a funny thing. It is difficult to make your first connection, but then a bit easier to make your second. As your network grows it gets easier and easier. This is one of the reasons why it isn't always a great idea to start with approaching the managing director of the company that you most want to work for. If you approach someone you don't know, you are essentially cold-calling them. As your network grows you will find that others know them and will be able to make an introduction.

You should start by looking around you and thinking about who you are already connected to and who might be useful to you. Start with your family, then move on to your peers, make use of the networking opportunities offered by the university and only finally start to move into the world beyond.

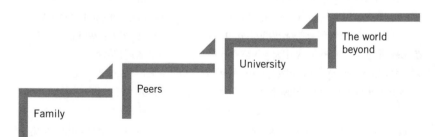

The world beyond

University

Peers

Family

Family

It might seem strange to view your family as part of your network. However, there is a long tradition of people being introduced to their first employer via their family. Think about your family and talk with your parents and siblings. Is there anyone that works in a field that you are interested in? If not, perhaps there is a family friend who can help. Maybe your Dad's boss or a woman in your Mum's book group works in the field that you've been desperately trying to get into.

You don't have to want to go into the family business to ask your family to help you. Sometimes just making a connection can be enough to get your network started.

Peers

The next place that you can look to start building a network is your peers. Every day you are surrounded by students who are interested in similar things to you and are probably looking for similar kinds of jobs. You can view these people as your competitors whom you have to beat to opportunities, or you can start to view them as a network. You are all going out spotting opportunities, finding out information and making connections. If you start to draw on each other's experience you will be stronger and more informed than you ever could be alone.

Furthermore, not everyone you know at university is going for similar types of jobs to you. Other people may be moving into very different fields, but if you ask them you may find that they have a parent or an uncle, aunt or cousin who can help you.

The best thing about your peer network is that it gets more valuable the longer you stay in touch with people. At the moment you know students, but in three years' time Elizabeth will be assistant head of marketing, Arif will be a lawyer and James will be about to finish his PhD. As everyone builds their career you will begin to see connections between their work and yours. Your connections will become relevant and useful in a professional context as well as a personal one. Keeping your university friendship circle together is a lifetime investment in your career.

The university

At the moment you probably think about university as the place where you study and as something that you are going to move on from when you enter the 'real world'. However, it is worth remembering that universities are a very big employer and are also organisations with very profound links to the wider world. Universities employ everyone from catering staff to theoretical physicists. If you look carefully, you'll find that universities employ people in marketing, press relations, management, schools liaison, law, accounting, human resources and a host of other roles. So, whatever you want to do, it is likely that you can find someone working for the university who is already doing it. It therefore makes good sense to build on the university's networks.

A good place to start is with the academics who teach your course. If you are thinking of going into research, teaching or some other kind of university work they will probably have advice and connections to offer you. If you are looking to branch out further they may still know people who could help you. So, if you are studying engineering it is likely that the academic engineer who is teaching you also knows some people who are practising engineers in industry. If you ask nicely they may be able to link you up.

Most universities also provide a careers service of some kind. Careers advisers are great people to talk about your future with because they can give you advice and help you to shape your thinking. In addition, most careers services also have people whose job it is to build links with employers, to organise careers fairs and set up placements for students. Accessing all of this professional help can really supercharge your network.

Universities also keep in touch with their alumni. Even the newer universities in Britain have been churning out graduates for 25 years. This means that wherever you go to university you should be able to find someone who graduated from your university who is currently doing your dream job. In most cases they will feel positive about their time at university, be happy to reminisce and probably be willing to give you a break because you have something in common. You should approach your university's alumni relations office and find out what opportunities exist to interact with alumni. Increasingly you can also find your university's alumni through a web search. In fact sites such as LinkedIn are designed to make finding these kinds of connections really easy.

Would you like to ... work in a university?

Working in a university can offer you some great career opportunities. It is also often quite easy to get started as a temp either while you are studying or immediately after you graduate. Doing some temp work in a university will allow you to 'see behind the curtain' and learn a bit more about how the university works as a business.

Most people who work in universities keep a close eye on the jobs.ac.uk website. This site lists lots of jobs at universities, from technicians and entry-level administrators to vice chancellors. A quick look around this site will tell you about the kinds of roles that might be available to you. The site also provides careers advice for people working in the higher education sector.

Universities tend to employ highly skilled people and to be quite keen on qualifications. While it is possible to work your way up as a bright graduate, many of the roles that are available in higher education may require further training and postgraduate qualifications.

Ambitious Futures is a graduate development programme designed to introduce graduates to different university roles while gaining a professional qualification (www.ambitiousfutures.co.uk).

Expanding your networks beyond the university

So far we've been talking about using the people around you to start building your network. Because networks run on trust and reciprocity this is one of the best ways to make progress fast. Nothing beats getting a recommendation from someone who really knows you. However, sometimes your immediate network won't do the job. If you are interested in working for NASA or in Parliament, it is quite possible that you don't know anyone who can link you up (although we'd bet that there is someone in your university who has a link to both of these). Sometimes you really want to branch out and meet some new people. After all, that is what networking is all about.

If you are looking to meet new people it is a good idea to jump on any opportunities that the university offers you. Most universities will organise regular employer talks, careers fairs and visiting speakers. Get into the habit of scrutinising these opportunities carefully and attending any that you think are useful. Always think about how you are going to talk to someone and get yourself known to them. You may want to take your CV or print some business cards, but it is probably better to find out their contact details and then follow up with an email.

Once you've used up all of the networking opportunities that your university can offer you, the next step is to start looking for opportunities beyond the university. A good place to look is professional associations, trade unions and other kinds of interest groups related to the job that you want. Pretty much every kind of job has a body that speaks for it. Many of these will also hold meetings in localities, and lots of them will have a special student membership rate. Join, volunteer and attend meetings, and pretty soon you will find that you know a lot of people who are working in the career that you are most interested in.

EXAMPLES OF PROFESSIONAL BODIES

Wikipedia has a brilliant list of professional bodies (see https://en.wikipedia.org/wiki/List_of_professional_associations_in_the_United_Kingdom) that covers everything from the Association of Chartered Certified Accountants to the United Kingdom Cast Stone Association. It is well worth looking through this list to find any that might be of interest to you. But to get you started here are some examples of professional bodies that you might be interested in.

The Chartered Institute for IT (British Computer Society) www.bcs.org

Chartered Banker Institute www.charteredbanker.com

Institution of Chemical Engineers www.icheme.org

The Law Society www.lawsociety.org.uk

Museums Association www.museumsassociation.org

If you look, you will find that there is an association for most jobs and that each offers you access to a ready-made network.

Networking online

Most of what we have said so far about networking can be applied online as easily as it can face to face. But for students and recent graduates online networking is particularly important. As a student you may not have the money and time to attend professional conferences and functions, but you can interact with people online.

When you interact online you need to try to apply the key principles of networking that we outlined earlier.

1. **Reciprocity.** Every time you contact someone online you are asking for a little bit of their time. They are far more likely to give that to you if they have seen you being generous with your time and trying to help others online.
2. **Equity.** Being online gives you the illusion that you can approach anyone. You could send a tweet to President Trump or Beyoncé. However, the higher up organisations you go, the less likely people are to have the time or inclination to get back to you. When you are networking online you should recognise the value that all people can bring. In many cases it may be a better strategy to contact someone who graduated last year and ask for their advice about your career. Being humble and respectful will go a long way and you may find that you build up a few advocates in some of the organisations that you are interested in.
3. **Authenticity.** The online environment is unregulated, so it is possible to say anything about yourself. When you are filling in a LinkedIn profile it would be possible to claim that you have got three PhDs and used to be the CEO of a Fortune 500 company. More commonly, people might tell a few little lies, perhaps boosting their grades or inventing a great-sounding job title. Unless you are a master criminal, lying about your career online or offline is always a bad idea. It is just too easy for a prospective employer to find out the truth either through a quick Google search, through checking out some of your wilder claims at interview or, more usually, just by following the maxim that if something sounds too good to be true then it probably is. Be honest and open and you will make contacts much quicker.
4. **Strategy.** You need to think carefully about the time that you are spending online. Surfing around LinkedIn and repeated clicking to 'connect' with someone won't really take you anywhere. When you approach someone

you should know why you are approaching them, what you are hoping they will do for you and what you might bring to them that could be useful. In general, people are willing to try to help you, but you need to try to make it easy for them by being clear about what you want.

5. **Tenacity.** Online networking requires a lot of patience. You may spend ages crafting a perfect email to someone that you have found online, only to find that they have retired and their email bounces back. You may find that many people don't respond to your questions and that others send back curt and unhelpful replies. Try not to get discouraged and keep at it. Networking online costs you only your time, so it is OK if only one in ten of your contacts pays off.

6. **Evaluation.** Online networking offers you the opportunities to experiment. Perhaps you might try to engage with people on Twitter for a week. If no-one is interested, switch to LinkedIn and have another go. Recognise when things are working and when they are not. You should also keep careful track of your network. Who is really being helpful to you, and how can you pay them back or acknowledge their help?

Top professional networking tools

- LinkedIn (www.linkedin.com) is the main tool that people use for business networking. You should definitely have an account and use it to make connections. It is also worth exploring what groups exist that relate to you interests.

- Twitter (https://twitter.com) is used for a wide range of purposes from sharing celebrity gossip to political campaigning. However, there are also a lot of professional groups that use Twitter to share news and ideas. Finding the groups that relate to your interests will help you to get to know some of the key people in your field.

- Blogs are key to the way in which professions communicate among themselves. Spend some time searching out the key bloggers in your field. If you are feeling more ambitious, start your own and use it as a way to get to know people.

- YouTube and Instagram are social networking sites that are particularly useful if you have visual or multi-media content to share.

- Specialist sites such as AngelList (https://angel.co – a social network for business start-ups) or Black Business Women Online (http://network.mybbwo.com) provide more focused forms of online professional networking. As with most things on the internet, there are more and more of these sites opening every day, so if you have a particular interest you may be able to find a specialist site that brings people together around this interest.

Maintaining your network into the workplace

Once you graduate your social and professional network is likely to change a lot. One way to think about your new job is that it opens up opportunities to build a new and more powerful network. Workplaces have a wide range of people with different levels of experience and seniority. Try to get to know as many people as you can and avoid just sticking with the other graduate recruits.

TIP: DEVELOP AND NURTURE YOUR NETWORKS

- Take advantage of opportunities to work with different departments, groups and individuals. Each new project you get involved in will open up some new contacts to you.
- Make the most of after-work drinks, parties and functions. While sometimes you might have had enough of work, being willing to socialise with your colleagues can get you better known and be a lot of fun. Be careful not to have TOO much fun in front of your colleagues, however!
- Find a friend at work (or even better a little gang). Having a few people that you can be honest with and confide in can really help you to make sense of the workplace.
- Find a mentor. You should actively look for someone who is more experienced than you, whom you look up to and who might be willing to help you. Approach them and ask if they would be willing to mentor you. Most people will be flattered and keen to help. Some companies even encourage or require you to do this.
- Look beyond the company. It is really important to build a network within your company, but in most industries it is just as important to know other people outside of the company. Going to industry events, professional associations and other sectoral bodies can really improve your knowledge of the industry and your reputation within it.

Finally, it is worth reiterating that once you go to work you shouldn't lose touch with your university network. Keep in touch with your friends, join the alumni association and update your old lecturers on what you are doing. You've spent at least three years building up this network – don't let it wash away just because you've moved on.

IN A NUTSHELL

- Building a network is key to your career.
- Networking can be challenging, but you are more than capable of pulling it off. It is just talking to people.
- Start networking with the people close to you and build out. It is amazing how much people you already know can help.
- Your university will provide you with a range of ways to connect to a wider network but you should also make use of professional associations and other opportunities.
- Networking online should be a key part of your networking strategy.
- Keep developing your network once you start working.

5 LOOK BEFORE YOU LEAP

Choosing a career direction is a very personal decision that can affect a lot of different areas of your life. It deserves careful attention and thought. Researching possible jobs, careers and employers will help you to make career decisions and will give you the edge in the graduate job market.

This chapter will help you to:

■ understand the importance of research

■ highlight key facts that you will want to learn in your research, including what questions to ask

■ identify practical and effective research strategies

■ deal with information overload

■ make an impact in recruitment practices.

Introduction

Being knowledgeable about your career options is crucial now and throughout your life. At this early stage in your career, research is of great importance. Without information about jobs, you will struggle to make a start on your career plans and applications. As you move on through your career you will probably find that some of your research will occur naturally as part of working in a particular industry. Your networks will expand and you will become connected to sources of useful information.

There will also be times when you will need to consciously apply yourself to the task of researching opportunities. It might be when you want to transfer to a different region or country, obtain a more senior position in your sector or perhaps try something completely new. The principles discussed below will help you to make sure that your information gathering is focused and complete.

Why is research so important?

In the context of our careers we use information for a few different reasons.

To explore and make decisions about jobs and careers we are interested in

A key part of successful career management is knowing what kinds of roles and responsibilities are out there for you. If you are at the beginning of your career journey, then this might mean looking at a whole host of options. You might be looking at different sectors, different sizes of companies as well as different types of roles. If you have already narrowed down the type of job you want or the kind of organisation you would like to work for, then your search might be more specific and detailed. All of this research will help you to consider what you want to do with your life.

To increase our understanding of our own value on the job market

Being able to match your skills, knowledge, experience, values and strengths with particular opportunities will help you to understand what kind of value you have on the job market. Your initial research will be a reality check in terms of what you can expect to earn or do directly after graduation. You might be surprised to learn that there is a lot of demand for new graduates in your field. Equally, you may find out that in order to compete you will need to have some distinctive experience or skills to bring to the interview table. Either way, you are better off as a candidate who has this information than you are without.

To enhance our knowledge and expertise in order to increase our chances of success when we apply for jobs

Your research will make you more effective in all of the recruitment activities that employers use. Whether you are writing your CV, submitting your application, taking part in an assessment centre or attending an interview – employers will want to know that you know something about them and this role. Your understanding and knowledge will demonstrate that you have a genuine interest in the sector and the job. Knowing that a company is about to merge with a competitor and understanding that your role would sit within a particular team within the organisation can make the difference between getting a job offer and not.

What questions should I ask?

Your research really begins with you. What do you want? What do you enjoy? What are you good at? We explored this in a lot of detail in our first chapter. In fact throughout this book we talk quite a bit about the importance of knowing yourself as part of building a rewarding and happy career (and life!). So, for the purposes of this chapter we are going to assume that you have done some of the internal exploring. It's time to look outwards!

There are three main areas you will want to look at in your research: the role, the company and the industry. You won't necessarily look at each in that order. Each has a relationship with the other and can't really be understood on its own. The important thing is to get started. Don't worry too much if you aren't 100% sure whether 'Merger and Acquisitions analyst' is the position for you or if the banking industry as a whole will suit you. Until you've done your research you can't really make a well-informed decision.

Would you like to ... work in investment banking?

A Mergers and Acquisitions analyst (M&A analyst) is a typical entry-level role in investment banking. As an analyst you will spend most of your time looking at financial data, assessing value and using this information to build pitches for clients. Essentially, you are offering professional advice to customers that will help them to determine their investment strategies and implement their financial transactions. You are likely to be working with large global companies, although this will depend on the size and prominence of the bank for whom you work.

Most (but not all!) graduates who enter this type of profession will come from a degree which has developed high levels of numeracy, such as one of the sciences, or from a business-focused degree, such as economics or management.

The salary for these roles can be high. Starting salaries around £30,000 are not unusual and the pay rises very quickly, making this type of graduate role financially lucrative. As a result, competition for a job as an M&A analyst in a top bank is fierce. If you are considering a role in investment banking, then it is a good idea to speak with someone in the industry to see if you are happy with the work–life balance you can expect from this kind of role.

A common route to a career in investment banking is to successfully obtain a summer internship in your penultimate year. So, ideally you'll be thinking about this career route early on in your studies. Otherwise graduate applications are normally online and recruitment will usually consist of assessment centre, interview and psychometric tests such as numerical and verbal reasoning.

For more information about careers in banking a useful source is eFinancial Careers (www.efinancialcareers.co.uk).

The role

Your first job after graduation will probably be an entry-level role. The expectation will be that you will be in this first role for a little while, maybe a couple of years, before moving up to a more senior role with different or additional responsibilities. So bear that in mind when you are looking at the job outline. Here is a list of 10 questions you should be thinking of when gathering information about a position. These are not questions you should ask the recruiter, they are questions you should be finding out about before you apply for a role.

- What are the entry criteria for the role? Are they asking for a particular degree subject or outcome? For example, a '2:1 in a numerate degree'.
- What are the core responsibilities and duties?
- What would a day in that role look like?
- What is the salary?
- When will the role start?
- Will there be opportunity for progression?
- Will there be additional training or study as part of the role?
- Where is the role based?
- What skills are listed in the job outline?
- What recruitment activities can you expect?
- Is my degree and/or work experience relevant?
- What type of contract will it be? (Permanent, fixed term, temporary, part time, etc.)
- What teams will the role work with?
- Will there be an opportunity to travel?

The company

Where you work will have as much of an impact on your happiness, well-being and success as the job that you do. You might work as an accountant in one firm and find the atmosphere dull and stifling, while the same role at another company might feel fresh and challenging. So, take time to read about each company before you apply and as part of your preparation for interviews.

Key questions you will want to answer include the following.

- What is the company's mission statement? (Many will list this on their own website.)
- How big is the organisation?
- What is the company's current business strategy?
- Who are their main competitors?
- What are examples of their most successful products or services?
- Who are the senior leaders in the company?

- Who are their clients or customers?
- What are the company's values and culture like?
- How would your role fit within the company?
- Where did the company come from? What is its history?
- What is the company's financial status?

TIP: KNOW YOUR ORGANISATION WELL

Conducting a SWOT analysis of the company can be an excellent way to prepare. Use your research to make a list of the company's Strengths, Weaknesses, Opportunities and potential Threats.

Strengths	Weaknesses
Opportunities	Threats

For more on SWOT analysis visit the Mind Tools website (www.mindtools.com/pages/article/newTMC_05.htm).

The industry and sector

We often talk about industry and sector as if they mean the same thing. But they actually have slightly different meanings. 'Sector' refers to large parts of the economy and it helps us to group together large numbers of organisations according to some major aspect that they share. Industry refers to more specific groups of organisations that have very similar business activities. So the term 'industry' provides us with more detailed specific information.

Depending on the type of job you are focusing on, the industry and sector may be extremely relevant to your choice of career. Working as a marketing director for a large software company in the private sector may be different from working as a marketing director for a local council in the public sector. Both jobs are in marketing, but while the work may be similar you will be serving different ends and mixing with different kinds of people. You may also find that pay and benefits vary as much by industry as they do by role. You need to think about how all of these factors will influence your enjoyment of your career.

- What are the major challenges facing the industry/sector at the moment?
- What will the industry/sector look like in 5, 10 or 20 years' time?
- Do they specifically need people in your field?
- How stable are jobs in this field at the moment? How about in the near future?

Get to know your industry

A PEST analysis asks you to think about the Political, Economic, Social and Technological factors affecting something that you are researching. Complete a PEST analysis of your selected industry to help you deepen your knowledge and understanding. Gather information on all of the Political, Economic, Social and Technological factors affecting the industry. You will find that this is a good way of identifying what you already know and where there are gaps in your knowledge.

Sector/industry	Political	Economic	Social	Technological
Finance	Impact of Brexit is yet to be determined	Recent economic downturn may result in increased regulation	Demographics – e.g. aging population will have an impact on pensions and investments	Concerns about keeping up with advancing new technologies

For more on PEST analysis and to download a template visit the Business Balls website (www.businessballs.com/pestanalysisfreetemplate.htm).

Research strategies

Being well informed will help to ensure that you have a good basis for making career decisions. You will be able to spot opportunities more quickly and will appear more knowledgeable when you go to interview. The process of research and using information is also a key employability skill that is applicable to most jobs. The internet has made the research process easier than ever before. In the past, researching career information required you to buy newspapers, visit libraries, research employer requirements and perhaps even learn to access complex statistics, but now the internet puts a vast amount of information at your fingertips.

If you want to search all social media for comments or references to something you can use Social Mention (www.socialmention.com). A word of caution: some of these sites can be an excellent form of distraction. Before you know it, you've spent 30 minutes searching for mentions of your best friend's dog or favourite pub in your home town.

Most job sites will give you the chance to create a profile and then receive information about jobs to your email inbox. Once you have specified the criteria for your jobs alert you will then be sent a confirmation email. The criteria might include things such as location, salary, job title and/or industry. Once you have confirmed your email and set up a password you will begin to be emailed jobs directly. Alerts work by emailing you any jobs that fit the criteria that you have specified. This can be tricky at first and you may find that you are receiving too many jobs (in which case you should log back in and narrow your criteria) or too few jobs (so you might need to be a bit more flexible, perhaps by lowering your salary expectations or increasing the distance you are willing to travel).

You should set up alerts for a few different graduate job sites. Here are a few that we recommend:

Graduate Recruitment Bureau (www.grb.uk.com)
Graduate Jobs (www.graduate-jobs.com)
Rate My Placement (www.ratemyplacement.co.uk)
Target Jobs (https://targetjobs.co.uk)
Fish 4 Jobs: (www.fish4.co.uk)

If you have already narrowed your search for a particular type of role, then these alerts will be of particularly good use to you. You will be kept informed of new roles and will be able to judge how the job market in your field is going. Are there a lot of roles on offer? Is the pay consistent? Is one company recruiting more than others?

Really Simple Syndication (RSS)

RSS is a technology that allows you to subscribe to a range of news feeds and to read them through an RSS reader (available from most app stores). RSS is declining in popularity, but it can offer you a neat way to bring all of your career-related information together. The key thing to look for with RSS is this symbol:

If you see that symbol, you can click on it and then paste the URL in your web browser into your RSS reader. An RSS reader is a web service or piece of software that allows you to bring together a range of different RSS feeds so that you can read them in one place. In essence it allows you to compile your own bespoke newspaper out of a range of things that interest you. There are lots of different RSS readers available and they tend to change fairly often. Wikipedia has a useful page (www.wikipedia.org/wiki/Comparison_of_feed_aggregators) which compares all of the currently available RSS readers.

Social media

Increasingly, websites are offering linked social media accounts. So, for example, the job board Go2Jobs offers linked Facebook and Twitter accounts that relate to specific areas (e.g. Crawley Jobs on Facebook and @Crawley_Jobs_UK on Twitter). If you live in one of the areas covered by this, you can subscribe to a relevant local jobs alert using whatever form of social media you feel most comfortable using.

Alerts are a vital part of the online career toolkit. Ensuring that key information is sent directly to you means that you don't have to remember to go and look for it every week. Receiving alerts can also help to keep you focused on your career building by regularly reminding you that there are opportunities out there.

Networks

The previous chapter focused on how you can build your networks and increase their effectiveness in terms of helping you to find meaningful work. As part of that strategy you should be using your personal networks to keep you informed about positions, companies and industry. In thinking about how to use your network as a source of information it is useful to learn a little bit of network theory. The sociologist Mark Granovetter[v] makes a really useful distinction between the people in your network with whom you have strong ties and those with whom you have weak ties. You have strong ties to the people you spend a lot of time with – family, close friends and classmates. You see them a lot and probably share a lot in common with them. In the context of career building, your strong ties can provide you with a lot of support. They are the kind of people you can ask to proof-read your CV or talk over whether to apply for a particular job or not.

Close friends who mean a lot to you are important, but they might not always be the best source of information about new opportunities. Your strong ties know all the same people that you know, they typically watch the same TV programmes, listen to the same music, read the same blogs and study at the same university as you. They are just like you, which is why you like them so much, but because of this they don't know very much that you don't know. On the other hand, your weak ties are more useful than you probably imagined: your cousin who lives a few hundred miles away, your old boss, that person you met at a training event last month. These people are all weak ties. They are typically less like you, they read, watch and listen to different things, study different subjects at different universities and live in different places from you. Because of this, your weak ties are likely to hear different information from you and are less likely to be competing for the same opportunities.

So, both strong ties and weak ties are important for career building, but weak ties are particularly important as sources of information. To make the most of your networks you should:

- audit your network. Who are you weak ties? Can you make better use of them?
- stay in touch. Make sure that you hold on to the contacts you have. Tools such as LinkedIn, Facebook and Twitter are really good for this purpose. They allow you to hold on to weak ties with minimal effort.
- think about what information you want and where it might come from. If you have decided that you want to work as a lawyer, you need to make sure that there are some lawyers in your network. This may lead you towards some strategic networking (see Chapter 4).
- tell (at least some) people what you are looking for.
- give as well as receive. As a member of a network you need to be a contributor, not just a taker. You should try to spot opportunities for other people and provide them with useful information. If you do this, they will notice it and return the favour.

TIP: MAKE LINKEDIN WORK FOR YOU

Have a look at your LinkedIn profile now. Does it indicate that you are looking for a new role in a particular industry? Make sure that your LinkedIn profile works for you. You can then message a few of your weaker ties to say hello and let them know of your current position. If they know you are searching for a graduate role in a pharmaceutical company, then the next time they hear of one they are likely to think of you. If they don't know, then you can guarantee they won't.

Making the most of your research

Now that you have a lot of information about the position, the organisation and the industry, you need to make sure you make good use of it.

Using information for career decisions – matchmaking

The big question is, how do you feel about the job now? Having looked at the responsibilities and skills related to the role, the values and status of the organisation and the current issues facing the industry – is it still a good match for you?

Yes! If the answer is yes, then that is great news. You can skip ahead to the next heading!

Not sure. If the answer is that you are not sure, then perhaps you need to do a bit more digging, either in yourself or about the position. Maybe you don't feel you have enough information to make a decision. Or perhaps you are looking for the elusive perfect job. We often talk about jobs and candidates resembling pieces of a puzzle – they should fit together. But in reality there is no such thing as a perfect fit. You should be looking for a good fit. But even if you aren't 100% certain that you are a good fit for the position, then you should consider continuing with your application. Getting a job offer is not a commitment in itself. The interviews and activities will be good experience, regardless of the end result. And you may find that as you move through the recruitment process you learn more about the organisation that helps you to come to a more confident conclusion – for or against!

No way! If your head and heart are both saying no, then this is probably not the role or company for you. If the job isn't a match in terms of skills, values, interests, rewards and duties, then not only are you unlikely to be successful in getting the job, you also are not likely to enjoy it. In the long run the job is probably not going to work out for you and you are probably not going to work out for the company. Best to go back to look at why you chose this role in the first place.

Using information to succeed in recruitment

Now that you are an expert on the job, the company and the industry, you need to use all of this information to your advantage. You will find that this can make all the difference at each stage of the recruitment process.

We've put together a table to remind you of how you should use your information at each of the usual recruitment assessments.

Recruitment stage	Use your information to ...
CV	Tailor your CV to the company. Use action words and skills examples that help to highlight your suitability for the role. Tailor your personal profile (if you choose to have one) to state that you are looking for a role in this industry.
Application	Provide examples of skills that link closely with those that are listed on the job outline. Use the STAR structure where relevant to ensure your answers are complete and have impact. See Chapter 7 for more information about STAR and preparing effective applications.
Interview	Be prepared with SWOT and PEST analysis so that questions such as 'What do you know about us?' and 'What do you think the industry will be facing in five years' time?' are easy! Use your knowledge of the sector to show that you are passionate and genuinely interested in the role. Be ready to answer 'Why do you want to work here?' Have a question ready that demonstrates your knowledge of the organisation. 'I noticed you are launching a new research project into young people and mental health issues. Is this something I might have an opportunity to learn more about and contribute to in the role?'
Assessment centre	Demonstrate the company's core values and culture through your behaviour. If the company states that it places a lot of importance on having a 'creative team that acts with integrity', think about how you can exhibit this in a group activity.

CASE STUDY

Marcia studied environmental science at university and is hoping that she will be able to put her knowledge to use in a graduate role in the sciences. She's pretty much narrowed it down to a role that focuses on sustainability. She discovered an interest in this topic while completing her dissertation, which focused on the social and economic impact of the exploitation of natural resources in northern Chile. Marcia set up a few job alerts on specialised sites and has found that there have been quite a few graduate roles featuring sustainability in the past month. It seems that it may be an area of growth in terms of environmental science jobs. She also found that she could work in a large variety of organisations and sectors in a role such as 'sustainability officer'. The breadth and potential flexibility of the role really appeals to her.

Marcia updated her LinkedIn profile to show what she is looking for in a graduate role. She then contacted her boss from her summer job at a youth camp and her Dad's friend who works in waste management in the local council at home.

Within a couple of weeks she had a few job options. The first was a graduate trainee role at a retail company (received by email alert), the second was a job as an environment education officer for a youth outreach project (received from her former boss) and the last was a job at the council in her home town as a researcher into waste management (received from her Dad's friend). She did some research and decided that she would apply to all three, even though the job with the highest pay was the one with the council.

Marcia was careful to tailor her CV and application to the different organisations, highlighting different skills and experiences according to the job role. She receive two invitations to interview, one from the retail company and one from the youth project. She used the PEST analysis to help prepare. Her research gave her insights into the potential career paths of both roles. She needed to consider what was most important to her and which organisation was likely to be able to give her what she was looking for in the short and longer term.

In the end, Marcia received two job offers. She chose to take the graduate trainee role with the retail company as she felt it would provide better training and career development. She still loved the idea of working with young people to educate them about important environmental issues, but she felt that she could still have the opportunity to do this in the future – and perhaps even organise her own education project through the company she was joining!

Would you like to ... work in environmental science?

If you are interested in working in the field of environmental science you will likely need to have studied a relevant science subject or to have a degree in environmental science itself.

There are a range of roles that fit well with a degree in the environmental sciences. You could work in education, research, emerging technologies, waste management or in an organisation that requires someone with insights into each of these areas. Your role might have a title such as environmental consultant, manager, project officer, education officer, planner, conservation officer, sustainability lead, etc.

An environmental education officer might expect to do things such as:

- develop and deliver educational programmes
- organise and promote environmental campaigns and events
- act as a point of contact and advice for local and regional groups, schools, volunteers and organisations
- analyse scientific data
- evaluate educational programmes
- manage budgets.

Earnings for this role might start in the £15,000–£20,000 range and could increase to £25,000–£35,000 for more senior positions. Salaries are higher for those with more responsibilities in large organisations.

Visit the Prospects website for more information about what you can do with a degree in environmental science (www.prospects.ac.uk/careers-advice/what-can-i-do-with-my-degree/environmental-science).

Search for jobs in environmental science on Indeed (www.indeed.co.uk) and on Environment Jobs (www.environmentjobs.co.uk).

IN A NUTSHELL

Information is a very important part of your career decision-making and your success in getting a job. To make the most of the vast amount of information that is out there you need to:

- understand the importance of research to your career development and success
- ask the right types of questions about the position, the organisation and the industry
- use a variety of search tools to make sure you don't miss out on information – and definitely go beyond the organisation's website
- make use of your existing networks, remembering that your weaker links might be more useful than you expect
- consider what the information you have means to you – use it to inform decisions about your next career move
- demonstrate your knowledge, passion and understanding at each stage of the recruitment process.

6 SHOULD I STAY OR SHOULD I GO?

Many students stay on after their first degree to do more study. But is this really a good idea? This chapter will examine whether postgraduate study will give you the edge and what course to choose.

This chapter will help you to:

■ understand what postgraduate study is

■ think about what you can get out of postgraduate study

■ understand the process of applying for courses and accessing funding

■ consider how to fit postgraduate study into your longer-term career aspirations.

Introduction

A lot of people have a good time at university. So far in this book we've been encouraging you to start thinking about what you are going to do after you leave university. However, you might feel that you aren't finished with university yet. Perhaps you want to get even deeper into your subject, or you feel that your career would be helped by having a few more qualifications. These are all good reasons for doing some further study.

Alternatively, you might feel that you want another year of university fun, that all your friends are in the year below you and that you want to graduate with them or that you just haven't got any other ideas about what to do next. These are common reasons for taking a postgraduate course, but in most cases we feel that they aren't very good ones.

The world of postgraduate study can be confusing. There are so many courses and qualifications that it can be difficult to penetrate what it all means. And what is the purpose of it anyway? Is it just for people who want to spend their lives as perpetual students or are there some jobs out there that require you to be postgraduate qualified?

In this chapter we are going to try to demystify the postgraduate world and help you to decide whether it is worth your engaging with it.

CASE STUDY

The end of the third year is approaching and John, Wendy, Aysia and Leo are all thinking about their next steps. Their department organises a lecture on postgraduate options. But this seems to mainly consist of a hard sell from the department as to why you should sign up for the MA that it runs. This is OK for John, who is bound for a first and whose tutor has told him that he should think about an academic career, but the others are not impressed.

Wendy is pretty keen to stay at the University of Grantchester because her boyfriend doesn't graduate until next year. She organises the rest of the group to visit the careers service and find out a bit more about the various option for postgraduate study.

Aysia discovers that if she wants to go into social work she is probably going to have to do some postgraduate study, while Leo finds out that there are a few options to study at postgraduate level once he starts work. In some cases employers will even pay. Worryingly for Wendy, she realises that the courses that she is most interested aren't offered by her current university (and so she might have to move away from her boyfriend after all).

They go back to their house with a pile of brochures and lots of opportunities. There are so many options! But then they realise that they haven't thought about how they are going to pay for another degree or whether postgraduate study is really worth it financially.

The more they find out, the more they realise that postgraduate study is not a way of avoiding making career decisions at all!

What is postgraduate study?

Postgraduate study describes a range of courses and qualifications that you can take after (*post*) you have completed a degree (*graduate*).

Most universities will produce a postgraduate prospectus. If you grab a copy of this you will probably find it a bit confusing at first. You will be offered MAs, MScs, MPhils, PhDs, EdDs and PG Certs, and PG Dips. Understanding what all of this means is not helped by the fact that there is relatively little regulation of all of these terms. This means that different universities might offer you a slightly different set of qualifications and mean different things by them. For example, it is fairly common to spot two pretty similar courses at neighbouring universities and to note that one is called an 'MA' and the other an 'MSc'. So, what does all this alphabet soup mean? And which of these qualifications is worth doing?

The following list should help a bit …

How it is referred to	What it means	What it is for	Example
PG Cert	Postgraduate Certificate	Accrediting shorter and less-intensive courses (perhaps lasting around a third of a year).	Postgraduate Certificate in Business Administration, The Open University
PG Dip	Postgraduate Diploma	Accrediting more intensive courses (perhaps lasting around nine months to a year). They do not usually involve doing any research.	Postgraduate Diploma in Deaf Education, University of Manchester
PGCE (sometimes PGDE)	Postgraduate Certificate (or Diploma) in Education	The initial qualification for teachers.	PGCE Primary Education, Edge Hill University
MA	Master of Arts	Awarded to those who can demonstrate a high-order understanding of the arts. Will usually take at least a year and include a research-based dissertation.	MA in History, Kingston University
MSc	Master of Science	Awarded to those who can demonstrate a high-order understanding of science. Science is broadly defined and may include some social science degrees and other degrees which require high numeracy. Will usually take at least a year and include a research-based dissertation.	MSc Finance, Imperial Business School
MPhil, MRes	Master of Philosophy and Master of Research	Research-based Masters that usually include limited amounts of teaching in favour of an extended dissertation. Confusingly, the MPhil is sometimes awarded to people who have failed to achieve a	MRes in Applied Health Research, University of Leicester

		PhD but who have completed a research project.	
LLM, MEd, MBA, etc.	Master of Law, Master of Education, Master of Business Administration	Specialist Masters which are closely tied to a particular field.	International and Commercial Law LLM, Kings College London
PhD	Doctor of Philosophy	A research-based course which requires you to develop a new piece of original research.	Almost all UK universities will offer a PhD
EdD, DBA, EngD, etc.	Doctor of Education, Doctor of Business Administration, Doctor of Engineering	Research-based degrees which are aimed at specific professional groups. They usually have a stronger taught component than a PhD and are often undertaken part time by working professionals.	Doctor of Education, University of Derby

The above list provides a starting point, but as you explore you will often find it a bit more complicated still. For example, if you start on a postgraduate certificate you might be asked if you want to study some more modules to turn it into a postgraduate diploma. Conversely, you might find that if you are unable to complete your Masters dissertation you may be able to exit the qualification with a postgraduate certificate.

Which one of these qualifications is right for you will depend on what you want to get out of it. Most people who take postgraduate qualifications do so for one of two reasons:

1. for the love of the subject and the love of learning
2. for career reasons.

In fact these two reasons are often closely aligned. You probably want to work in a field that you are interested in, so studying something interesting will hopefully lead you in this direction. So, thinking about how you are going to spend the rest of your life and what kind of work you might do is at least a factor in making a choice about postgraduate study. Because of this all postgraduate course decisions are essentially career decisions.

We think that there are two main routes that you can take: the academic route (where you focus on an academic subject and open up the possibility that you might want to become a lecturer or researcher) and the professional route (where you focus on a job that you want to do after you have finished the course).

The academic route

For people who are primarily interested in the love of learning and the love of their subject there are a large range of postgraduate courses. There are postgraduate courses (usually Masters) on offer that correspond to every undergraduate degree that you might have taken. And there are a host of more specialised courses. So perhaps you did a degree in English and really enjoyed learning about Victorian novelists. Well, in that case the University of York's MA in Victorian Literature or Culture would appeal to you.

Masters level study also gives you an opportunity to change direction. You may have studied chemistry at undergraduate level and be passionate about the environment. In that case you might be interested in the fact that the University of East Anglia accept students who have completed an undergraduate degree in Chemistry for its MSc Environmental Sciences.

TIP: START WITH YOUR OWN UNI

Universities are usually pretty keen to sign students up for Masters courses. If you are interested in a course it is well worth talking to the admissions tutor even if you are not sure that you meet the requirements. They will often find a way to get you on the course.

If you are pursuing the academic route you are starting down a particular career path. Many of the academics teaching you will assume that you want to follow in their footsteps. This usually means completing your Masters and then taking a PhD.

A typical academic career path

Masters	You take a research-focused Masters for 1 year.
PhD	You undertake a PhD specialising in a particular topic for 3-4 years.
Postdoctoral researcher	You spend anywhere between 1 year and your whole career working as a researcher. As you get more experienced you may have more control over your research agenda.
Lecturer/ Senior Lecturer	As you get more experienced it is common to start lecturing. This often means getting paid more, but, as you are teaching, you get less time to spend on research.
Associate Professor/ Professor	Senior academic roles include associate professors and professors. These roles are usually better paid and have more freedom to focus their research on their interests.

At each stage of an academic career you will find that it becomes more competitive. So a lot of people have a Masters, fewer have PhDs, fewer still manage to get a postdoctoral position and so on. It is worth talking to some people who are currently on this career path before you start moving down this route yourself.

However, there are a lot of different career paths that can emerge from this kind of route. Some will be about using your subject expertise, others will be about using your skills in research and analysis and still others will just be general roles where the employer understands the value that postgraduate qualifications can bring.

When you are applying for programmes that take you down an academic route you should ask what the graduates of the programme are doing now. This kind of information will help you to think about what you might want to do once you have completed the course.

Would you like to ... be an academic?

Academics are involved in teaching, research and administration and are employed by universities or other kinds of research institutes. If you want to become an academic you will usually require a PhD, although in more applied disciplines, e.g. education, nursing or social work, it is common for academics to be recruited from practice and then to gain a PhD while teaching at a university.

An entry-level lecturer will probably start on around £30,000, but an experienced professor might earn anywhere upwards of £60,000. The levels of pay will depend on both the subject taught and the institution that you work for.

For further information on research and academic careers visit the Vitae website (www.vitae.ac.uk) or Jobs.ac.uk (www.jobs.ac.uk).

My tutor says that I should do a PhD. Should I?

Sometimes you may find that an academic takes you aside and suggests that you should think about studying for a PhD. They may have opportunities to offer you, such as the 1+3 Awards (which fund a one-year Masters followed by a three-year PhD).

This can be very flattering and offer you a great opportunity. But you should think carefully about how you respond to this. The academic who has approached you sees some potential in you but they are also trying to steer you into a particular career path. It may have been the right one for them but that doesn't mean that it is necessarily the right one for you.

Think carefully about these kinds of opportunities and decide whether they are right for you. If you would make a great academic you would probably also make a great something else. Don't let flattery blind you to what you really want to do with your life.

The professional route

Most Masters degrees are focused on training you for some kind of professional role. Even the academic route discussed above is essentially a training route for academic and research careers.

Some examples of postgraduate courses that take you down a particular professional route

Course	Institution	Professional pathway (who might take this programme)
Advertising and public relations management MSc	DeMontfort University	Designed for people who want to work or who are already working in the marketing and advertising industry.
Purchasing, logistics and supply chain management MSc	University of Bedfordshire	Designed for people who want to develop specialist skills within business around purchasing, logistics and supply chain management.
Postgraduate Diploma in Community Specialist District Nursing	University of Cumbria	Designed for qualified nurses who want to upskill and specialise in district nursing.

As these examples show, professional-route postgraduate courses cover a wide range of topics and professional areas and appeal to a range of different audiences. Some are designed for people who come straight from undergraduate study, while others are aimed at people who are already in practice or who are looking for a career change.

It is important to research carefully the professional-route courses that you are considering.

10 questions that you should ask about all professional-route postgraduate qualifications that you are interested in

1. What profession does this qualification relate to? Is it a specific job or a wide occupational area?
2. Is this qualification the only way to become part of that profession? Are there alternative qualifications? Is it possible to learn on the job?
3. Does this qualification actually give you a licence to practise? Some postgraduate qualifications qualify you completely, others provide credits towards accreditation by a professional body and still others do not actually qualify you for anything. Before you pay your money, you should find this out.

The exact status of postgraduate qualifications in every profession and occupation is constantly changing. As the demand for roles goes up and down and as universities and other providers of qualifications develop new routes to professional status, these requirements shift. It is important that you do some research into the professions that you are interested in and find out what the current situation is. Doing a postgraduate degree is never going to hurt your prospects but it may not always be the fastest way to get qualified for a particular role.

Can I compensate for a poor degree?

Earlier in the book we talked about the fact that graduate recruiters are often looking for a 2:1 or higher. If you completed your degree and ended up with a 2:2 or worse you may be tempted to take a postgraduate degree to boost your employability. This may work in some situations but you should ask yourself the following.

- Is your 2:2 actually going to be the disadvantage that you fear? Some graduate recruiters are less interested in your grades than others.
- Are you sure that you will do better in your Masters than you did in your first degree? Think about what prevented you from getting a better mark and consider whether you are going to be able to perform better if you take a more advanced (and probably more difficult) degree.
- How are you going to make the most of the extra time that you are buying to build your employability? Getting another degree might help a bit, but you can really enhance your career by also taking the opportunity to network, to engage in extra-curricular activities and take up opportunities for placements and work experience.

Will it guarantee me a higher salary?

In general, people with a postgraduate degree are more likely to find a job and earn a higher salary (perhaps £2,000–£3,000 more on average).[vii] However, these general statistics disguise a lot of variation. For example, it is clear that a Masters pays more if you already have some work experience in comparison to when you do it straight after your first degree. It will also depend on what subject you do and in what job you try to use your new qualification.

An influential report that was published about this talked about 'masters with a purpose'.[viii] We think that this phrase provides a good summary of what the evidence tells us about doing a Masters. If you know what you want to do and why, and you have thought about how it relates to your future career, a postgraduate degree can really enhance your employability. But if you just wander into something, the chances are you won't be any better off than you were at the end of your first degree.

ACTIVITY 6.1

Pros and cons of doing a postgraduate degree

Now we've explained what a postgraduate degree is and discussed the reasons why people do them you should be in a good position to think about what you should do.

Take a piece of paper and draw a line down the middle. List all the reasons why you should do postgraduate study on one side (Pros) and all the reasons why you should not do it on the other (Cons).

Pros	Cons
I'd like to carry on at university	It is expensive
I'm interested in a career that requires a Masters	I think that it might be good for me to work for a while before I do more study
…	…
…	…
…	…

Put down whatever comes into your head. Don't worry about whether it seems to be an important or a silly reason.

Once you've finished making the list put it down. Come back the next day and review it. It will help you to decide whether this is the right choice for you. The longer list is not necessarily the one that you should go with, but the process of listing pros and cons will help you to think this through.

It is also worth thinking about what you will do if you don't do a postgraduate course. Having nothing better to do goes some way towards justifying spending the next year building up your qualifications, but we are not sure that it is the best reason. Be careful not to drift into postgraduate study because you are too lazy to look for a job.

Fitting postgraduate study into your life

You should embark on postgraduate study with some care. However, the right course for the right person can offer some major opportunities. But how do you deal with the practical aspects of finding, applying for and studying a postgraduate degree?

Finding the right course

In general you should have a pretty good idea of the kind of course you are interested in by the time that you get to postgraduate level. If you aren't sure what sort of thing to study, we'd suggest that you go and work for a bit while you figure it out. However, even if you have got a very good idea of the course that you want to do you will probably find that there are tens (or even hundreds) of universities that provide the course that you are interested in. So how to choose?

In general, if you can imagine it, there will be a postgraduate course somewhere that will cover it. A good place to start is Google, and just try searching on subjects that you are interested in + 'masters' or 'postgraduate'. Another way is to identify a few institutions that you are interested in and then to have a look at their postgraduate prospectuses (usually online these days). Below you will find a number of postgraduate course-search tools that may also help you to find some courses that you might be interested in.

Course-search tools

- Complete University Guide: Postgraduate www.thecompleteuniversityguide. co.uk/postgraduate
- FindAMasters /www.findamasters.com
- MastersCompare www.masterscompare.co.uk
- Postgrad.com www.postgrad.com
- Postgradute Search www.postgraduatesearch.com
- Prospects – Search postgraduate courses www.prospects.ac.uk/ postgraduate-courses
- UCAS postgraduate search https://digital.ucas.com/search

Start by making a long list of courses and then start crossing out courses that don't fit or aren't in the right location. Once you've got it down to about five courses do some more detailed research and see what you can find out about them.

For now, it isn't important to choose a single course and it is probably a good idea to start applying to more than one.

Should I stay at the same university?

Lots of people start from the assumption that they should stay at the same university to do their postgraduate study. After all, your friends are all there and you know that the tutors are good.

This can often be a good decision, as setting up in a new town can take a lot of time and effort – but we'd advise you to consider some other options before you just go with what you know.

You should probably start by finding the best course for you. Postgraduate study gives you an opportunity to trade up and get a degree from a more prestigious university. It also gives you the chance to find the course that most closely matches your interests and the department that graduates the most successful students. Take the time to investigate all of these issues before you decide where you want to study.

Should I study abroad?

Taking a postgraduate degree abroad can offer you some exciting opportunities. It will give you a chance to travel and to experience a new country, to meet new people and to offer your CV some glamour. Employers are bound to be impressed if you say that you took a Masters at Harvard, the Sorbonne or Leyden. From a personal point of view, it can make a lot of sense as you are going to be paying for your postgraduate degree and living costs anyway, so why not combine it with an adventure?

In general, we think that taking the opportunity to study abroad is well worth thinking about. But before you pack your bags there are a few issues to consider.

■ Does the university that you are thinking about teach in a language that you are really fluent in? Linguistic ability is key to your chances of success in all postgraduate study, so you need to be confident in speaking, listening and writing in the language that you are going to be working in. This having been said, you might be surprised at the number of international universities that are now teaching in English.

■ How long is the postgraduate course that you are interested in? One of the reasons why UK Masters degrees are so popular with overseas students is that they are shorter than those offered in many other countries. A typical UK Masters lasts only a year (with teaching often covering only nine months). Masters overseas tend to be two years or more.

■ How does studying abroad relate to your career aspirations? If you want to pursue a career of globetrotting, then studying in Boston or Tokyo is a great way to build experience and make connections. But if you've got your heart set on finding a job in Chesterfield you might do better to look at universities that are more local. A good postgraduate degree will open up a new network for you and you should choose a university where this network is relevant to where you ultimately want to work.

Should I do it full or part time?

For most people the experience that they have had of being a student is pretty much a 24/7 one. Yes, you might have worked a part-time job, but your primary focus was probably on being a student and completing your course.

The experience of learning and taking any kind of course can change once you leave university. After this point, if you want to take a course you usually have to juggle it with work (and family and social life and so on).

Most universities offer most of their postgraduate courses in both full-time and part-time forms. Sometimes they will also offer distance learning and e-learning versions of the programme, to allow people to learn flexibly. One of the reasons why they do this is because most people aren't in a position to take a year or more out of work, and so offering flexible courses increases the market of people who can take up postgraduate courses.

It is possible to see taking a postgraduate course full time as a bit of a luxury. If you can afford it or can find a way to make it happen you will probably find it easier than if you have to try to balance it with a job. However, there are also some upsides to taking a postgraduate course part time. If you are working while you study you will be building work experiences and networks that, if you are working in a related field, may inform your study and help to develop your career. The coming together of theory and practice in part-time study can be a powerful learning experience – as long as you can find enough time for both.

Applying for postgraduate study

When you applied for your undergraduate degree you probably used the UCAS system. UCAS helps to manage the huge number of applications to universities and tries to ensure that the universities all get filled and that all applicants find somewhere to study.

Postgraduate applications are a bit more chaotic. In general you apply to each university that you are interested in on an application form that they have designed and go through a different process with each place. We'll get to the application bit in a minute, but first, how do you find where to study?

Choosing a course
We've already discussed making a long list of courses by doing some research on the internet. Once you've got to this stage you should start doing some more intensive research online or by phone. You should ask to talk to someone and find out whether the course is what you are really after.

When you've found a course that you are really interested in, arrange to go and visit the university where you will be based. It is important to see the place where you will work (and maybe live) and it is even more important to talk to some of the staff who will be teaching you and students who are currently studying on the course. Most departments that you are likely to be applying to will be willing to help you to organise a visit and talk to a few relevant people.

Applying for a course
The process of postgraduate application is fairly straightforward. Most universities will have an online form for you to fill in. Deadlines for applications are usually a bit more flexible than with undergraduate courses, but it is usually a good idea to stick to the deadlines advertised. You may find that some courses offer multiple entry points in the year, so if you have missed the September start you may be able to start in January or April.

Universities will publish their entry requirements in their postgraduate prospectus. In many cases they will actually be fairly flexible and open to negotiating these kinds of requirements (within reason). The hard requirements (grades etc.) are important, but you will ultimately need to convince the university of the following things.

- You can complete the course. You have the time, motivation and ability to do all of the things that are required.
- You have the money/funding to pay for the course.
- You understand what the course is about and can articulate why it is of interest to you.
- You can connect the course to your career aspirations. This doesn't mean that you have to know exactly what you are going to do after you finish, but you have got to be able to explain why it makes sense in career terms.

If you can convince the university to which you are applying of these four things it will probably accept your application – although clearly some courses are more competitive than others.

TIP: DON'T PUT ALL OF YOUR EGGS IN ONE BASKET

It is always worth having a plan B (and probably C and D as well). So, when you are applying for a postgraduate course you should probably apply for more than one. Try to be honest with people as soon as you can about what your actual intentions are. Once you have been accepted and have decided where you are going to go, then inform all of the other courses that you won't be enrolling with them.

It is also a good idea to apply for a few jobs alongside your applications for postgraduate study. Once you get a few offers, it will put you in control and give you a new perspective on your decision.

Gaining funding

Studying for a postgraduate course is going to cost you some money. The average postgraduate course will probably cost around £8,000, and the fees are rising as they come into line with the £9,000 a year that undergraduates now pay. However, depending on the course, you may find that you could be paying a lot more or a lot less.

In addition to your course fees you will have to pay for living costs, and in some cases additional expenses such as buying books, field-trip fees and so on. So, before you embark on a postgraduate course it is important to spend some time budgeting and thinking about the financial implications of doing the course.

There are a range of ways in which people usually fund themselves through postgraduate study.

- **Your own money.** Maybe you are rich, have an inheritance or trust fund or, alternatively, have been working and saving. In this case, you may choose to invest your money in your own development.
- **Bank of mum and dad.** Depending on your family situation, you may be able to borrow or get given some money by your family to help with your postgraduate education.
- **Your employer.** Lots of employers are willing to pay for their staff to take postgraduate qualifications. Sometimes this will be built into your contract when you are first hired (e.g. in accountancy). Other people may have to spend a few years working before they are in a position to ask their employer to support them through postgraduate study.
- **Borrow the money.** The government has recently brought in postgraduate loans along similar lines to the undergraduate student loan. At the time of writing these can cover up to £10,280 for students in England. The devolved governments have developed similar schemes, but it is important to check your eligibility. In the past it was common for people to apply to the bank for a career development loan to fund postgraduate study. In general, the government loans give you a better deal, but it is worth investigating all of the options.
- **You get a grant.** For a few lucky students there are opportunities to access funding for postgraduate study. This may be because you are able to secure a grant from a research council, because you are training for an occupation that the government is trying to incentivise people to go into (e.g. science teaching) or because you have some other characteristic that makes someone interested in encouraging you to take a particular route. Not all grants will necessarily cover the full fees and living costs of taking

a postgraduate degree. Sometimes they might be relatively small amounts of money; for example, some universities offer a discount for their own graduates who want to continue on to postgraduate study.

TIP: FIND OUT THE FACTS OF FUNDING

Postgraduate funding is changing a lot at the moment. The Prospects website (www.prospects.ac.uk/postgraduate-study/funding-postgraduate-study) has a lot of good, up-to-date information. However, this is something that it is really worth spending some time researching and talking to your university's careers service about. You are going to be spending a lot of money on this, so it is worth making sure that you get the best deal.

Keep thinking about your career

If you do decide to start a postgraduate course you should remember that this is an opportunity for you to build your career rather than a cast-iron guarantee that all your dreams will come true. In most cases courses last a year or less and you will need to start thinking about your next step pretty much as soon as your course starts.

As with your undergraduate degree, it is really important to make sure that you do as well as you can in terms of attainment. However, you should also be very focused on grabbing career opportunities where you find them and building your network. If you do this your postgraduate degree will really pay off.

IN A NUTSHELL

- Postgraduate study is not for everyone. Don't just drift into it because it seems easy.
- You should think carefully about what you want to do and what you hope to get out of it.
- You need to decide whether you are going down the academic route or the professional route, as this will guide your choice of postgraduate degrees.
- Research your options carefully. Consider a range of courses and universities and really weigh up the pros and cons of each.
- Think about how you are going to fund postgraduate study and what your return on investment will be.
- Remember that postgraduate study is a step on your career journey rather than a way to avoid career decisions.

7 SUCCESSFUL APPLICATIONS AND INTERVIEWS

This chapter will outline typical recruitment practices used by employers and provide strategies that you can use to come out on top.

This chapter will help you to:

- understand typical recruitment processes

- understand the timing of recruitment processes

- perform effectively at different types of assessment and selection

- avoid common pitfalls

- access other sources of support.

Introduction

Not many of us enjoy writing lengthy applications or look forward to an interview. But these recruitment hurdles serve a purpose. They help companies to define what they are looking for, and candidates to articulate what they have to offer. They are a two-way process where you have the opportunity to choose them just as they have the opportunity to choose you. Thinking positively about the process and knowing what it is for can make a big difference to your success and confidence.

What are employers looking for?

One of the things that can really knock our confidence or worry us when it comes to applications and interviews is the unknown. *What is the employer looking for from me? What question will they ask next?* A good way to get over your worries is to try to put yourself in the shoes of the employer.

CASE STUDY

Bob has 112 CVs and applications for the graduate trainee role. He has to review them and make a short list for telephone interview by the end of the afternoon. He knows he can't read them all fully so he starts by grouping them into piles. Pile A is candidates who meet the basic criteria (2:1 or above in any degree subject, 300 UCAS points[1]). Pile B is candidates who do not.

Pile A now has 89 applications. Next he gets rid of any applicants who didn't bother to attach their CV. Bob figures that if the candidate couldn't be bothered to follow instructions then he doesn't have to bother to read their application. Now he has 67 applications.

Next Bob does a skim through for typos. He has a rule – more than three typos or grammatical errors and he puts the application on Pile B. It's surprising how many small and big errors he finds. Now he has 39 applications. This is a more manageable amount!

[1] The way that UCAS Tariffs are calculated changed in 2017. This means that students who started their studies after this date will find that employers are looking for the new Tariff score. Visit the UCAS Tariff calculator for more information www.ucas.com/ucas/tariff-calculator.

Next Bob reads through his 39 applications and CVs. He is using an assessment matrix. This is basically a table with a list of all the criteria, skills and experiences that were listed on the job outline. Bob gives each application a score out of 10 in each section. A score of 0 means there is no mention, 5 means there is a mention but it isn't very convincing, 8–10 is an excellent score – the candidate has explained their experience very well, with an example that clearly evidences the skill and has impact and succinct detail. Once he has marked them all he will be able to decide where the cut off between pile A and pile B will be. Bob finds this is an easier way of working out which applications he thinks are the best.

This brings Bob down to 17 applications. There are two graduate trainee positions available, so Bob thinks 17 is a good number. The next stage will be to invite the students to a telephone interview and then an assessment centre.

Recruitment is often a mass exercise, so employers need to find ways to move from a lot of applicants to a few as quickly and efficiently as possible. Bob's time is expensive. So are interviews and assessment centres. It is important that graduate recruiters are able to identify high-quality talent quickly so that their resources are not spent in vain.

Your job is:

1. don't give the employer an easy reason to put your application in pile B (spelling mistake, not following instructions, applied for wrong role)
2. do give the employer the evidence that they need in order to keep your application in pile A.

What does graduate recruitment typically look like?

Getting a graduate job is no different to getting any other kind of job. Anyone who wants to pay you to work for them will want to have a way of figuring out if you are the right person for the role. The techniques that they use to do this, whether they include application forms, tests, role play or formal interviews, are all just tools to help the recruiter (and you) to come to a sensible decision.

TIP: GRADUATE JOBS AREN'T ALWAYS CALLED GRADUATE JOBS

Most graduate jobs will not have the word 'graduate' in the title. There are a great many large, well-known organisations that regularly recruit hundreds of new candidates to their graduate schemes. There are even more companies seeking degree holders to fill roles that are not explicitly badged as graduate. Both kinds of organisations will want to select the best possible people – which is where your amazing application and outstanding performance at interview comes in!

When it comes to hiring new graduates, not all organisations use the same recruitment practices – but they all use something. What is helpful is that (a) we know that there are some common practices and (b) organisations are usually very open about the practices that they use.

Here are the most common stages of recruitment:

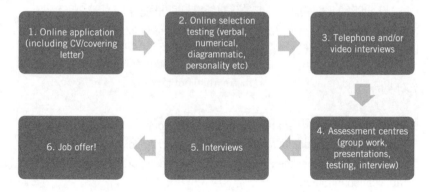

Most organisations will engage in at least Stages 1, 5 and 6. Some, usually the larger organisations with more resources, will use all six stages. Occasionally these are all merged together at an assessment centre.

TIP: CAREER MANAGEMENT IS FOR LIFE ... NOT JUST YOUR FIRST JOB

You will make use of your application and interview skills now and forever! You may have picked up this book because you want to find a job after graduation ... but your next job is not going to be your last job. Managing your career is a valuable and rewarding *lifelong* skill and your ability to present yourself well in recruitment is a key part of that. In fact, as you move on in your career you will likely find yourself on the other side of the interview table and your understanding of what a good candidate looks like will become even clearer.

Timings for graduate recruitment

The number of stages will usually have an impact on the length of time recruitment can take. You might apply to a company in October and not reach the final stage of recruitment until March. More recently there is a move to shorten the length of time that recruitment takes, as employers can see candidates beginning to disengage or to accept other offers over a longer period of time. We have also seen a rise in the use of telephone and online video interviews, which offer an inexpensive method of selecting (or de-selecting) candidates early on in the recruitment process.

Larger organisations tend to begin their recruitment as early as August or September for employment in the following June/July. A lot of companies will close their recruitment near the end of the year (December or January), which means that a lot of students will be completing applications in the first half of their final year. Your university will be aware of this and will be offering workshops, careers fairs, employer presentations, mock interviews and guidance from September to January.

Recruitment doesn't come to a grinding halt, though. Some organisations will continue to recruit throughout the year, only closing their applications when they are 'full'. And of course throughout this process some students will decline job offers, which means that a company might re-open its recruitment or re-visit applications to fill its vacancies.

Small to medium-sized organisations might need to be more reactive or flexible in their approach to recruitment and this can affect both the timing of their recruitment and the way that they recruit. They might, for example, find that they have a surplus of funds at the end of the financial year (April) and this allows them to recruit for more positions. Or the success of a new product line might mean that they need to invest urgently in new resources to support the business. In this case they might forgo an assessment centre and instead rely on application and interview stages only.

When it comes to the 'when' of recruitment, the following are the key messages.

1. Be aware of the deadlines for the companies or sector that you are interested in.
2. Start early – you *can* be one of those students who secures a job offer in October, leaving you free to enjoy your final year of studies without further pressure of applications and interviews!
3. Make use of the support offered on your campus in the autumn term.

Here is an example of a recruitment timeline and what you probably should be doing at various points in your studies.

Month/year	What you need to be doing
First year of your studies	Investigate careers from your subject Find your careers service Prepare your CV Get involved in something!
Summer after your first year	Organise some form of paid or unpaid work experience
Start of your second year	Apply for summer internship and placement year opportunities Attend careers fairs and presentations Consider study abroad and Erasmus programmes Get involved in something else! (Or deepen your involvement in something.)
November/December of your second year	Summer internship and placement scheme applications begin to close.
Summer after your second year	Organise some form of paid or unpaid work experience.
Start of your final year	Apply for graduate roles.

November/December	Graduate schemes begin to close in November and December. *When do applications close for your favourite jobs?*
October–March	Psychometric testing, assessment centres and interviews take place for applications you have made.
March–June	Small to medium-sized enterprises (SMEs) are likely to be advertising for graduate roles.
May–June	Some large graduate schemes may re-open applications to recruit to unfilled positions.
After graduation	Graduate internship opportunities may still be available through your university careers service.

Would you like to ... work in recruitment?

Recruitment consultants are professionals who match people to jobs and jobs to people. They often specialise in a particular sector (e.g. finance) or type of work (e.g. secretarial). Working in recruitment is a very client-centred job. You need to be good at building relationships and be aware of the expectations of the employer and potential candidates. It can be a varied job with a typical day involving telephone interviews, managing social media alerts, employer site visits and agreeing contract details.

In terms of salary, as a trainee you can expect to earn a fairly standard graduate starting salary of between £15,000–£20,000. This will rise over a short period of time. Senior, experienced recruiters can expect annual salaries of £35,000 and beyond. For more information about working in recruitment visit the graduate recruitment bureau website where you can read a variety of profiles from those working in recruitment: www.grb.uk.com/work-in-recruitment/why-work-in-recruitment.

The best preparation for any stage of recruitment is to research what you can expect and then to practise. So, for the rest of this chapter we will take you through each of the stages of recruitment, explaining:

1. what is involved
2. why recruiters use them
3. common errors and how you can avoid them.

Stage 1: CV, cover letter and application

Your first opportunity to communicate formally with a company might very well be through your CV, cover letter and application. So it needs to give an excellent first impression. Before you start drafting your CV or application, do some research. Think about why are you applying to this company. What does the role have to offer to you? What makes you a good candidate for this company and job? Also, try to put yourself in the shoes of the employer. Why are they recruiting? What are they looking for? What do they NOT want to hear from you? Once you have answers to these questions, then you are ready to make a start.

CVs

Your CV will normally cover one or two full pages. There are many CV resources and examples that you can consult online and in books (see the 'getting more help' box below for examples). A good overall structure will include the following items.

Name and contact details – Keep it simple and up to date. There is no need to include personal information such as gender, age or nationality. Avoid embarrassing or unprofessional email addresses (e.g. drunkmike666@gmail.com).

Personal statement – This will be a few short lines about where you are now and what sort of position or opportunity you are looking for. Your personal statement can be changed to suit the application so that your CV is tailored for each job application.

Education – You should start with your most recent education first and work your way back. Include specifics such as awards, grades or particular modules/courses if you think they are relevant.

Work experience – Again, you will begin with your most recent experience. Depending on how much work experience you have, this section may be very long or very short. You can leave out work experience that you don't feel is relevant or significant if this section is looking rather long.

It is more common for students to struggle to fill this section, so do make sure that you are including all of your work experience, whether it is paid, unpaid or directly related to the role in question or not. See Chapter 3 for more help on this.

Transferable skills (optional section) – If your work experience section is looking a bit sparse, then you can add another section detailing some relevant transferable skills that you have developed through your studies and work and other experience. This will make it possible for you to make the most of the work experience you have and to make it very clear to the employer that you have some of the key skills that they seek. Make sure that you have done your research beforehand to identify some of the skills that they are looking for.

Additional skills/achievements – This is a section where you can make an employer aware of any specialist skills that you bring to the table. Languages, IT skills, positions of responsibility, awards that you have received – all of these can help to bring your CV to life and give the employer a better sense of what you have to offer.

References – You can include named referees and their contact details (make sure you have their permission first!), but it is not expected. Most CVs will finish with a statement declaring that 'References are available upon request'.

Do I still need a CV in the age of LinkedIn?

LinkedIn is a free online resource that recruiters use to find candidates and that candidates can use to link with others professionally. It is essentially your online CV. For the time being you are still likely to need to have a word-processed CV to augment your applications, but LinkedIn has a lot to offer. We would recommend that you engage with LinkedIn early on in your job search. It can be a good way to link up with organisations and to develop helpful networks. It is also a great way to keep your CV up to date and available to you at all times – it's never stuck on a laptop at your parents' house or lost on a missing USB stick.

You can learn more about using LinkedIn and other social media sites in our *You're Hired! Job Hunting Online* guide.[ix]

A sample CV

Shayla Smith
657 Rockford Close, Leicester, LE4 789
Mobile: (44) 09677951187
Email: shayla.smith645372@email.com

I am an ambitious and committed English graduate with a flair for creative projects and building effective relationships. My work experience in retail sales, media, tourism and fundraising has helped me to develop key transferable skills such as customer service, communication and project management. I am seeking a graduate role in media that will make the most of my skills, knowledge, passion and potential.

Education

2014–2017	Brilliant University, Manchester, UK
	BA (Honours) English Literature 2:1
	Modules included: Early American Literature, Creative Writing, Victorian to Modernist Literature, Independent Research Studies, Writing for Publication, Theory in Practice, Global Literatures
	Dissertation Topic: Language in Modern Literature – A study in the development of language in 20th century popular fiction.
2012–2014	Lovely Sixth Form, York, UK
	A levels: English (A), Biology (B), Maths (B), Sociology (B)
2006–2012	Super Secondary School, York, UK
	GCSEs: English Language (A*) English Literature (A*), Maths (A), Geography (A), History (B), Science (B), French (B), ICT (B)

Work Experience

June 2016 – June 2017   **RAG (Raising and Giving) Fundraising Co-ordinator,**
Manchester University Students' Union, Manchester

- Led a team of 12 students in running six charity fundraising events across the academic year.
- Successfully raised over £33,500 in charitable funds, breaking the previous university record by more than 15%.
- Chaired regular meetings and delegated work to team members as appropriate.

July 2016 – Sept 2016   **Tour Guide, Visit York, York**

- Responsible for leading small groups of tourists around Manchester city centre for regular two-hour tours, promoting events, amenities and areas of historic interest.
- Developed bespoke tours for specialised groups (e.g. disabled persons, children and historic society).
- Received consistently high feedback from clients and groups.

Oct 2015 – June 2016   Assistant Editor, *Manchester Student Voice*
- Collated and edited creative writing pieces from over 25 students over the course of 2 themed issues of the magazine.
- Project managed the launch of the magazine with a university wide event and social media campaign.

Oct 2014 – June 2016   Customer Service Advisor, PhoneCo, Manchester
- Assisted customers with mobile phone sales and queries.
- Managed stock orders and organisation of window and shelf displays.
- Handled cash and card sales and completed end of day close of unit.
- Inducted and trained three new members to the sales team.

Relevant Skills

IT	I am a confident user of all Microsoft Office packages and have a strong grasp of editing programmes. Working in retail sales required me to use various database and payment systems, which I was able to learn quickly and easily. I am an avid user of social media and write my own blog: www.ShaylasStories.blognow.com.
Communication	My time spent as a tour guide saw me listening to and communicating with a diverse range of people. I am able to write and edit written work to suit different audiences and enjoy presenting to large and small groups.
Teamwork	I enjoy working with others on projects. Fundraising for RAG required regular meetings, co-ordination of activities and organisation of events – all of which involved working effectively with others in the team. As a result we exceeded our target for the year.

Achievements

May 2017	RAG was awarded the **Student Union Society of the Year** for our record breaking fundraising, of which I played an integral role.
June 2012	I was short-listed for the York Youth Creative Writing Competition and had two pieces of work published in the 2012 York *Young Minds Creative Writing Anthology*.

Interests

I enjoy reading and creative writing and am a regular contributor to online writing forums. When not reading or writing, I enjoy playing tennis, swimming and trips to the theatre.

References

References are available upon request.

Cover letters

Your CV should be accompanied by a cover letter. The purpose of a cover letter is to provide the polite, written introduction that your CV can not. Your cover letter should:

■ be word processed, short, polite and to the point
■ introduce who you are and why you are contacting the individual/organisation
■ explain why you are a strong candidate for this position
■ invite the employer to view your attached CV for more information
■ thank the employer for their consideration
■ include date, names (yours and theirs), your contact details and signature.

TIP: GETTING MORE HELP WITH CV AND COVERING LETTER

Use your university careers service – it will have samples, a CV review service and one-to-one appointments to help you. You can usually continue to access these services after graduation too!

Samples of CVs and covering letters can be found in lots of different places on the internet. If you do use a sample, make sure that you make it your own. Some sites we recommend include:

○ Prospects: www.prospects.ac.uk/careers-advice/cvs-and-cover-letters
○ Target Jobs: https://targetjobs.co.uk/careers-advice/job-hunting-tools-downloads
○ Graduate Recruitment Bureau: www.grb.uk.com/graduate-cv
○ There is also another book in this series that is focused entirely on writing a great CV (*You're Hired! CV: How to write a brilliant CV*)

Applications

Most organisations will require you to complete an online application. These will vary in detail and platform from one company to the next, but normally they will all want to receive much the same kind of information. Unlike your

CV and cover letter, your application provides the employer with a standard way of looking at all their candidates. They will be looking to see that you meet their more basic criteria (level of education, grades, background of study etc.) and how you compare when asked a set of more detailed questions about your experience, motivation and knowledge.

The first set of questions on an application is normally fairly factual: education, work experience, qualifications, name, contact details etc. Next you will normally find some more in-depth questions aimed at getting to know you a bit better, such as the following.

- Why do you want to work for us?
- What makes you an excellent match for this position and this company?
- What skills and experience do you have that you can bring to the role?
- What has been your greatest achievement?
- Give an example of when you have had to deal with multiple projects and competing deadlines.
- Tell us about a time when you have dealt with change. How did you deal with it and what was the outcome?

It is a good idea to try to structure your written answers so that they tell your story succinctly and with impact. A very popular structure is one that is known as the STAR technique. STAR stands for Situation, Task, Action and Result.

On the following page we give an example of the STAR technique and how to apply it.

Application question: Tell us about a time when you worked in a team to achieve a goal

S = Situation – What was happening?	I worked with my university volunteering group to arrange educational events for primary-aged children. We wanted to involve them in some fun science experiments to try to engage them in science and maths early in their education. As a chemistry student I knew science and maths could be exciting and I wanted to bring that excitement to others.
T = Task – What needed to be achieved?	We knew we would have to work with schools, the university, the insurance and safety team and our lecturers in order to come up with a programme that would work for everyone.
A = Action – What did you do?	I organised our first meeting and suggested we allocate roles and responsibilities across the team. I took on the communication with local schools so I had to work closely with the publicity officer and the person developing the programme of events. I made sure that we met regularly and that the teachers always knew exactly what to expect from us and when.
R = Result – What happened as a result? Would you do it differently next time?	We held three separate events in the spring. A total of 127 Year 4 and 5 children came to the events. We asked the children and teachers to evaluate the programme. Their evaluation was really good and they have asked for the programme to be repeated next year. In hindsight I think we underestimated how many different people had to be involved in order for the project to work. We had to have twice as many meetings as originally planned and the first event was very stressful as we had to do a lot at the last minute. Next year I will start the planning and meetings at least a month earlier and I will involve people at an earlier stage. We are seeking funding for the project through an employer now, so I'm pleased with our success and the contribution I made to it.

Using this format will help you to structure your answer clearly and will ensure that you give a good account of your experience in your answers. Be sure to use the word 'I' in your answer. Although your work might have been done in a team the employer will want to understand what your specific contribution has been. If you can include figures or facts it can add a lot of impact to your answer.

STAR can also be very helpful in interviews, so we will re-visit STAR briefly in that section.

Common errors in CVs, cover letters and applications

This book will help you to understand what you should do to be successful. Sometimes it can be helpful to know what not to do, so that you can avoid common pitfalls. With that in mind, here are some reasons why candidates are not selected at this stage of recruitment.

What went wrong	To avoid this
Applied for the wrong role	Do more research.
Errors in spelling or grammar	Spell check everything with both a word processor and a friend.
Significantly over or under the given word limit	Improve your attention to detail and have a friend double check your application.
Did not target application or cover letter to the organisation or role (or even worse, sent a targeted cover letter to the wrong organisation!)	Do your research, target your applications and have a friend double check your applications before sending them off. Fewer, better-quality applications will be more successful than many poor-quality applications.
Did not articulate skills and background well and/or did not match the job specification	Use STAR and the job specification to ensure that you have written effective answers that meet the criteria in the role.
Did not 'sell' skills and experience effectively	Remember that employers are interested in many different forms of work experience and skills – not just those that appear to be directly relevant to the role. Include your time spent working with children at summer camp, your stint at a fast-food joint, your voluntary work etc.
Did not answer the question	Use the STAR technique and re-read your application – have you answered the question asked?

TIP: GETTING MORE HELP WITH APPLICATIONS

Use your university careers service. It will have resources you can use and application workshops that you can attend. It will also likely offer a one-to-one appointment to help you. You can usually continue to access these services after graduation too!

Stage 2: Online selection testing

Tests used for recruitment and selection are also referred to as psychometric tests. Recruiters use psychometrics in the early stages of recruitment to help them find the candidates who best meet their requirements. These tests are standardised and objective. They are a cost-effective method of filtering the pool of candidates. Not all recruiters will use psychometric tests, it will depend on the job and the company. The good news about this stage is that employers are typically open about the tests they use and it is almost always possible to improve your scores with practice. So, you have no excuse not to ace your test!

There are two main groups of psychometric tests:

1. aptitude/ability tests
2. personality tests.

The type of test that you are asked to complete will depend very much on the role for which you have applied. If the role requires a lot of numeracy, then it stands to reason you will be asked to complete a numeracy ability test. The tests will normally be set up so that you view one question at a time, with multiple-choice answers to select. Your test will be timed and you may find that the questions increase in difficulty as you progress. You may struggle to answer some questions in the time allotted. Don't let this worry you. The recruiters will be looking for a particular benchmark across all of their candidates. You won't necessarily know what that is until after the test has been completed and you have heard from the recruiter. Many tests are deliberately set to be difficult to complete in their entirety in the time allocated.

1. Aptitude and ability tests are used to determine a range of your personal attributes. Some seek to establish your capacity to learn something new, others to look at your knowledge and skills in a particular area such as numeracy or problem solving. Examples of aptitude and ability tests include the following.

Verbal or logical reasoning: assesses your ability to understand and interpret written information and make decisions about opinions or arguments based on the information provided.

Numerical reasoning: assesses your mathematical ability and how you interpret numerical data, charts, statistics, graphs etc.

Diagrammatic or abstract reasoning: assesses your ability to recognise patterns in a sequence.

2. Personality tests are designed to help employers to assess how you might behave at work, how you work with others, how you respond in different situations and what you are like as a person.

Personality tests are not tests that you can practise at to improve your score. A company that uses personality tests will be looking for particular character strengths and indicators and it is best not to second-guess what these are. It may be matching your outputs with previously successful recruits to the job. You can practise these tests to ensure you feel comfortable completing them, but don't expect to 'improve your score' the way that you can with other tests. If your answers reveal that your natural strengths don't match those needed for the role, then it is quite possible you would not be happy or excel in the position, at least not now. We talked a bit about examples of personality tests and their limitations earlier in this book in Chapter 1.

In addition to personality tests and aptitude/ability tests you may find that you have been given a spelling or error-checking test or a test to see how well you can use a software programme such as Microsoft Excel. But these would typically be administrated later in the recruitment process, at an assessment day or interview. At that point you should be in a good position to predict the type of tests that may be used.

Common errors in online selection testing

When candidates are not selected at this stage of application, the following are often the reasons why.

What went wrong	To avoid this
Didn't reach the benchmark for the test	Practise for each test – it is possible to improve on your results with practice (for most tests). Make sure that you are in a quiet room where you will not be disturbed.
Technical problems	While recruiters may be sympathetic, the chances are that the fault is not with their system. Check that you have full battery power on your device and you have turned off any disruptive notifications such as email/ Facebook etc. If something goes wrong, try not to panic. Take a screen shot and make the recruiter aware of the problem after the test is complete.
You weren't able to concentrate	Make sure that you are in a quiet location and you won't be disturbed. Make sure that you have eaten, had a good night's sleep and that you have water on hand to keep hydrated.

TIP: GETTING MORE HELP WITH ONLINE SELECTION TESTING

Use your university careers service. It will have workshops and a subscription to free practice tests that you can use.

- Use other online practice sites such as Graduates First (https://www. graduatesfirst.com/), Psychometric Success (http://psychometric-success.com/) and jobtestprep.co.uk (https://www.jobtestprep.co.uk/).
- There is also a book in this series (*You're Hired! Psychometric Tests*) that focuses specifically on psychometric tests at a greater level of detail than is possible in this book.[x]

Stage 3: Telephone and video interviews

More and more recruiters are using telephone interviews and video interviews. Both represent a cost-effective method of selecting candidates for the next round.

A telephone interview will be exactly what it sounds – an interview conducted over the telephone. These interviews will have standard questions and will normally be fairly brief, perhaps 15–30 minutes long. You should expect some questions about your suitability for the role, your motivation for applying to this role/organisation and your knowledge of the industry/sector. As the interview is on the telephone you can use notes to help you with your answers. Avoid reading out answers, as this will sound rehearsed and unnatural. For more on what kind of questions you can expect, look further on in this chapter at Stage 5, where we outline different types of interview questions and provide examples.

Video interviews are becoming more popular as the technology that supports this is becoming more cost-effective and accessible. You will be sent a link that will launch a programme on your computer or mobile device. There will normally be a short introduction, including some instructions for completing the interview recording.

This type of interview *is not* conducted in real time with a live interviewer. The questions are likely to be asked through a video recording of an interviewer, or read out and written on screen. You will be given a question to answer, a minute or so to prepare, and then the software will begin recording your response to the question. The types of questions will be similar to those that you will be asked in a telephone interview. The big difference of course is that you are being video recorded and there is unlikely to be a real-time connection to the interviewer. You will need to dress and act as you would for a live interview.

Common errors in video and telephone interviews

When candidates are not selected at this stage of application the following are often the reasons why.

What went wrong	To avoid this
Not able to answer questions about motivation for the role or knowledge of the industry effectively	Do more research Practise – your university will have mock interview services available.
Technical problems or interruptions	Make sure that you are in a quiet location and you won't be disturbed. Check that you have full battery power on your device and you have turned off any disruptive notifications such as email/Facebook etc. If something goes wrong, try not to panic. Make the recruiter aware of the problem after your interview is complete/submitted.

Did not articulate skills and background well and/or did not match the job specification	Use STAR and the job specification to ensure that you have prepared effective answers that meet the criteria in the role.
Did not answer the question	Use STAR technique when answering questions. Use written prompts to aid you as necessary, but be careful not to read from a script.
Lacked confidence, appeared overly nervous	It's normal to be nervous, and nerves can actually help us to perform well. If your nerves are getting in the way, then find out what relaxation techniques can help you – breathing techniques, visualisation, meditation etc. Remember to smile, as this will significantly affect how you come across in the interview. You will get better at all of this with practice.

TIP: GETTING MORE HELP WITH TELEPHONE AND VIDEO INTERVIEWS

■ Use your university careers service. It will offer mock interviews and often have a room that you can reserve to practise and conduct your video or telephone interview.
■ Request and reflect on feedback that you get from employers and professionals.

Stage 4: Assessment centres

If you've reached the assessment centre stage, then you have done extremely well. You have probably done a good job of showing that you have the potential to do well in the role and that you are genuinely interested in the organisation. Great!

Assessment centres are used to give interviewers the chance to see how you perform under challenging circumstances and how you interact with others. You will often be asked to work in a group on a timed project. While you are working on the project you will be observed by a small panel of people who will be taking notes. The end result of the project might be a series of recommendations or a project idea that your group must present to the panel. It is important to remember that your observers are looking for how you interact with others and how you approach a group task. They might not be looking for the person with the loudest voice, the best ideas or the quickest solution. They might be looking for someone they can imagine working with in the future, someone who helps to keep the group on task, someone who displays good leadership or listening skills.

Assessment centres can be a lot of fun. At this stage you have done your research into the company, you know why you want to work there and you have given some solid evidence that you would be able to make an effective contribution. So try to approach the group activity with a positive attitude and be the best version of yourself.

Recruiters sometimes like to use assessment centre days as a chance to do more than a group task observation. The chances are they have invited you to attend for a large part of the day, possibly all day, so they may want to include other selection tests to make the most of your visit. Most commonly this is additional or repeated psychometric testing and/or a face-to-face interview. They may ask you to undertake an in-tray (or e-tray) activity. In an e-tray assessment you are given a set period of time to work through and deal with a series of email messages. They will be looking to see if you can prioritise and delegate work appropriately, as well as how you deal with stress.

It is important to remember that the company are probably looking to appoint more than one person from their assessment day exercise. So, while you want to perform well, you don't necessarily need to view all the other candidates as your direct competition. It is possible for more than one of you to shine and for more than one of you to receive a job offer. Being the best version of yourself might mean showing how well you can listen to, support and encourage others in your team, and that is ok!

Common errors in assessment centres

When candidates are not selected at this stage of application the following are the often the reasons why.

What went wrong	To avoid this
Did not contribute	Remember that the observers can comment only on what you have contributed. If you don't say very much they will have less evidence to collect about you. Consider in advance what roles you feel comfortable taking on in a group activity. Could you offer to take notes, keep track of time or present the summary?
Did not answer the brief for the task	Has your group answered the task? Sometimes conversations get off track, or the group will follow an exciting idea that doesn't actually answer the brief. Refer back to the brief to ensure that your group are focused on the intended outputs.
Ran out of time	Timing is designed to be an issue for these tasks, in order to simulate a high-pressure environment. Ensure that your group are mindful of the time throughout the tasks. Delegate someone to be a time keeper, or volunteer yourself.
Did not participate in the presentation	Again, the observers will be able to report back on your contributions only if you have in fact contributed. Prepare yourself for doing presentations beforehand by practising in front of a mirror and others.
Did not display effective teamworking skills	Observers are looking for evidence of good interpersonal skills. What will they see and hear from you? What feedback have you had from others about your teamworking skills? Participate in mock assessment centres and act on feedback you receive.

TIP: GETTING MORE HELP WITH ASSESSMENT CENTRES

■ Use your university careers service. It will have practice sessions and advice.

■ Have a look at *You're Hired:Assessment Centres: Essential advice for peak performance* for more tips.

■ Ask for and use the feedback you get from the observers.

Stage 5: Interview

An interview is a fairly high-cost activity for any organisation. Senior people will be taking the time out of the business to make themselves available, rooms will be booked, resources created and checked, travel costs and hotels often reimbursed and so on. If you have reached this stage of the recruitment process the chances are good that the company is hoping you will be a good fit for the organisation. It may be hard to believe, but they will probably be silently cheering you on from the other side of the interview table and giving themselves a pat on the back for selecting such a great candidate.

Throughout the recruitment process you've been doing research and building up your understanding of the industry, the organisation and the role. You know why you want the job and you have some evidence to show that you are able to contribute to the company. Your interview will be about reiterating all of this. It will be a chance for you to show your personality a bit more and to talk in more depth about yourself and the job. You can normally expect an interview to last anywhere from 30 minutes to an hour. There will usually be a panel of two to three people interviewing you and taking notes, some of whom you may already have met through other recruitment activities.

Interviews are also a chance for you to get to know the people with whom you will be working and the culture of the company. You will be able to ask more specific questions about the type of work you will be engaged in and what kind of training and career progression you can expect.

A good performance at the interview will start with good research. So, be sure to review all of the research you have done already and brush up on things in the news that may be relevant to the organisation and sector.

Of course you will want to look professional, relaxed and self-assured. Make sure that you feel comfortable and confident in your chosen outfit. Get plenty of rest the night before and plan your travel so that you can arrive in good time without feeling overly stressed. Eat something beforehand and stay hydrated with plenty of water.

What kind of questions will they ask?

Recruiters may use different formats for their interviews. You might find that the employer is very transparent about the type of interview that they use. If not, it is best to prepare for a range of questions from each of the following formats.

Below we give examples of interview types and five sample questions that you can expect from each of these question types. Typically an interviewer will use a few from each question type.

General questions about suitability and motivation

These are questions that most interviewers will ask, no matter what overall style of interview they are using.

1. Why do you want this job?
2. What makes you a good candidate for this role?
3. Where would you like to be in five years' time?
4. How does this role fit with your overall career plan?
5. Tell us about how your previous work experience and studies will have helped to prepare you for this position.

Questions about the industry/organisation

Companies want to know that you want to work for them in particular. They also want to know that you understand what working in their organisation or industry means.

1. What are the biggest challenges facing our industry at the moment?
2. Tell us about something you have read in the news recently that relates to our organisation.
3. Why do you want to work for our organisation/company?
4. What, in your view, is our organisation's biggest strength/weakness?
5. Which of our products or services do you value and why?

Competency-based interviews

In a competency-based interview recruiters are asking you to give them evidence from your work experience and studies that illustrate a particular transferable skill or ability. These questions are very common in graduate recruitment. Look for the key skills and competencies listed in the job description and prepare answers based on those skills. The STAR technique works very well with this type of questions.

1. Tell us about a time when you worked with others to solve a complex problem.
2. We are looking for an effective communicator. Can you give us an example of when you have changed your communication style to suit different audiences?
3. Influencing skills will play an important role in this position. Describe a situation in which you used your influencing skills successfully to convince others of your viewpoint.
4. Tell us about a time when you dealt with a difficult customer. How did you resolve the situation?
5. We are looking for rational, logical thinkers. Can you give us an example of when you have approached a situation rationally and logically? What was the outcome?

Strength-based questions

In recent years more recruiters are using strength-based interviews. This may be a reaction to the commonness of the competency-based questions – students and graduates have become more adept (or competent!) at answering competency-based questions and recruiters feel they need to use different/additional tools to help discover the talent they are looking for. Strength-based questions are designed to get to the heart of who you are. It may be harder to prepare for these questions as they are not asking for past experiences so much as they are looking to discover your natural strengths, likes and behaviours.

1. Describe your perfect day.
2. What qualities would you bring to the organisation?
3. What is your biggest strength/weakness?
4. What do you enjoy doing in your spare time?
5. Tell us about something that you are particularly proud of.

Technical questions

These types of questions are normally used when you are applying for a role that requires particular technical skill. Sometimes you may be asked to complete a technical test alongside your interview to help assess your ability.

1. How has your academic background prepared you for the work you would do in this role?
2. What experience do you have of Excel/customer relations management systems/software?
3. What are your technical qualifications?
4. What languages have you programmed in?
5. What do you understand about the process of usability testing?

An excellent way to prepare for interviews is to write out your answers to each question and practise saying them aloud. Then put your notes away and ask a friend to pose the questions to you. You will see quite quickly which questions still need more practice and which you feel confident and poised in answering.

Random questions

Sometimes interviewers will ask questions that seem a bit random. They might not seem to relate directly to the job. Normally these questions are included for one of two reasons (and not just to entertain the panel after hours of interviewing!) (1) They want to see how you react when presented with something unexpected and what that reveals about your personality. This can help them to understand you better as a person and to see if you might be a good fit with their team. (2) They want to see your approach to problem solving. They might for example want to see if you can think rationally about how to solve an unusual problem – even if you can't give them the exact right answer.

1. How many oranges would fit inside this room?
2. Describe yourself in just three words.
3. If you were on a desert island, who would you want to invite to be there with you?
4. Will the sale of mobile phones in the UK increase in the next five years or decrease? How might you find out?
5. Name five uses for a paper clip – other than using it to clip paper together.

Your questions

Most interviewers will ask at the end of the interview if you have any questions for them. You should have at least one prepared in advance. This is a chance for you to find out something more about the organisation or the company. You can also use this as an opportunity to demonstrate your interest in the sector. It is not the right time to ask about contract details such as holiday, pay or hours.

Examples of questions to ask.

1. Will there be an opportunity for further study or training as part of this role?
2. Will I be involved in your latest project/campaign? (Show what you know about their latest products and services.)
3. Where is the role based?
4. What do you like most about working here?
5. When can I expect to hear from you and what will be the next steps?

While you might not get all of these questions, you will likely be asked something similar, so it makes sense to have prepared some of these in advance. The STAR technique discussed earlier in this chapter is a helpful, simple structure to follow when thinking about how to answer interview questions.

If you get asked a question and you are not sure how to answer, try not to let it bother you too much. Politely ask the interviewer to repeat the question. Interviewers are likely to repeat it more slowly, giving you a bit more time to think. They may also rephrase the question which may aid your understanding. You can say that you want to think about the question for a moment. A short pause is absolutely fine and will demonstrate that you are taking the questions seriously.

Common errors in interviews

When candidates are not selected at this stage of application the following are often the reasons why.

What went wrong	To avoid this
Nerves got the better of you – spoke too quickly, rambled, mind went blank	Being nervous is normal and is often part of performing well in a stressful situation. But if your nerves are getting in the way of showing you at your best, then you need discover relaxation techniques that work for you – breathing techniques, visualisation, meditation, etc. Try to slow down your speech to avoid appearing too nervous and to avoid rambling. If your mind goes blank, excuse yourself and move on. You can come back to a question later on in the interview if necessary. Practising will build your confidence, so if you have a poor interview experience, reflect on it and move on!
Did not answer the question	Use STAR technique when answering questions. Ask the interviewer to repeat or rephrase the question if you are unsure.
Did not build rapport	Smile and make eye contact, as this will help you to build a relationship with the interviewers and will help you to relax. Practise introducing yourself in advance. How will you say goodbye at the end of the interview? A strong beginning and end will help to build your confidence and will make a good impression.
Asked inappropriate questions	Now is not the time to negotiate salary, holiday, a corner office or special hours. Stick to questions that demonstrate your engagement, such as career progression, new projects or issues affecting the sector.

TIP: GETTING MORE HELP WITH INTERVIEWS

- Use your university careers service. It will offer mock interviews.
- Ask for and use the feeback you receive after the interview and from professionals.
- There are plenty of other books that focus on interviews, including one in this series! (*You're Hired! Interview: Tips & Techniques for a brilliant interview*).

Stage 6: Getting a job offer

Congratulations, you've been offered the job!

For many candidates, there doesn't feel as if there is anything to consider at this stage – you got what you wanted, so you just need to accept the offer and bask in your success.

But there are three things we would like you to remember when you are offered a job.

1. Get your offer in writing as soon as possible. An email outlining the hours, salary and position would suffice. Is it what you expected?
2. You don't have to say yes immediately. You can ask for a day or two to consider the offer.
3. You can counter-offer, if you think you are worth more or would like some additional conditions included (opportunity for training, honouring of a holiday you have already booked, guarantee of a particular location, for example). Of course you need to remember that they can always say no.

You can change your mind about a job. Just because you have said yes to a job offer does not mean that you have sold your future to that company. But if you do feel that you have made the wrong decision, then be sure to act responsibly. Be polite, courteous and apologetic. Inform the organisation as soon as you can that you have changed your mind.

Whatever your plans, always assume that you might want to be able to return to the organisation one day, and act with this in mind. This is an excellent rule to follow throughout your career.

TIP: GETTING MORE HELP WITH JOB OFFERS

If you are unsure about how to respond or negotiate, visit your university careers service for advice.

On reflection

Applications, testing, assessment centres and interviews can be stressful but they can also be revealing learning opportunities. And you may even enjoy yourself! Take some time to think about what your experience has taught you. Have you discovered a hidden talent or passion? Are you more (or less) convinced that you are heading in the right direction in terms of your career? Has some of the feedback you've received surprised you? Have you discovered alternative opportunities, career paths or people who can help you?

What will you do next as a result?

IN A NUTSHELL

- Knowledge is power – know the processes that make up recruitment for the sector, job and organisation you are interested in. Do research so that you know what to expect and can prepare.
- Practise at each stage of recruitment. Get feedback from friends, family and professionals and practise again!
- Make use of different sources of support to give you the best chance of success.
- Remember that recruitment is a two-way process – use it to learn more about a job role, an organisation and a sector to help you decide if the role is a good match for what you want.
- Use recruitment to deepen your learning about yourself and your potential new job.

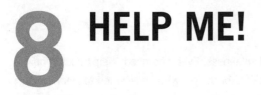

8 HELP ME!

We all need help now and then. Ask anyone who is a bit further on in their career and they will no doubt be able to tell you a few stories of people who helped them to get where they are. Sometimes it is easy and natural to get the right help, maybe through family or friends. Other times it might feel as if you are quite alone and you will need to search for someone who can help you.

This chapter will help you to:

■ recognise when you might need help

■ understand what kind of help is available on campus and beyond

■ use the help that is available effectively

■ identify web resources that can help.

Introduction

Asking for help is not a sign of weakness. Everyone needs help at some point. In fact employers are often looking for people who know when to ask for help. Being self-reliant and tough is great, but ploughing on when you've got no idea what to do is just senseless. Employers would much rather hire someone who asks for help than someone who makes a mess of things because they are too frightened or proud to ask for help.

But asking for help isn't always easy. You need to recognise that you need help, to find someone who can help you and then pluck up the courage to ask them for help. This can be embarrassing, but you need to recognise that asking for (and giving) help is a key skill in your career.

Recognising that you need help

The fact that you have picked up this book shows that you have some idea that you might benefit from help and information when it comes to your career. This kind of self-awareness will benefit you enormously throughout your life. Here are some clues that might indicate that you could use a bit of extra support:

- feeling lost and unsure about what the next step might be
- being repeatedly unsuccessful in recruitment (perhaps not getting past the assessment centre stage, for example)
- feeling panicked at the thought of completing an application or going for interview (feeling nervous is perfectly normal, but if your nerves are stopping you from getting started, then you would probably benefit from some help)
- feeling concerned about your qualifications or lack of work experience
- receiving feedback that you don't understand.

If any of the above describe how you are feeling or have felt about your career development, then you would almost certainly find that accessing additional help and support would be useful.

Who can help me?

The list of people and organisations who want to help you is quite long! Let's explore the different types of help and different types of people/organisations offering support.

University career support services

Your university will have a wealth of support available for you to tap into. Your first port of call should probably be your university careers service. It could be called the Careers Service, the Career Development Centre, the Employability Support Unit or any of a host of other weird and wonderful titles. But you're almost a graduate, so we bet that you can spot it when you find it. Slightly more difficult to find are those career services that are part of more general student support services, but again, you should be able to find them. If in doubt, ask someone who works for the university and they should be able to point you in the right direction.

Once you've found your university's student support service you will find that they offer a wide range of services. Think about the kind of help that you need and then use the table below to help you work out which kind of support will be most useful to you.

I want to ...	Services that your careers service is likely to offer to support this
Find help in thinking about what comes next	One-to-one guidance Web resources such as questionnaires and information about potential career paths
Learn about different types of jobs, employers and sectors	Employer visits, workshops and presentations Careers fairs Information about what graduates in your discipline have gone on to do
Get some work experience	One-to-one guidance Online jobsites (including your university's own online site) Competitions Volunteering programmes Skill-development awards University-supported internships
Succeed in the recruitment process	CV and application tips Mock interviews

	Workshops and mock assessment centres Web resources and applications such as practice psychometric tests, interview-recording software etc.
Prepare for starting work	Workshops One-to-one guidance
Start my own business	One-to-one enterprise and entrepreneurship guidance

Would you like to ... be a careers adviser?

It may seem odd for a book on careers to be encouraging you to think about becoming a careers adviser, but as we've both had enjoyable careers in careers we thought that it might be worth you thinking about it.

Careers professionals are involved in helping people to think about, plan for and take action in their careers. They can work in schools, colleges or universities but may also work with unemployed people, in companies as part of human resources or as freelancers.

Salaries start from around £18,000, but specialists or managers may earn £50,000 or beyond. The higher education sector tends to offer better salaries but will often require more experience.

Careers advisers can train in a number of ways but it is becoming increasingly common for them to have degree- or Masters-level training.

For further information see Prospects (www.prospects.ac.uk/job-profiles/careers-adviser) or visit the Career Development Institute (www.thecdi.net), which is the professional body and provides advice on training and qualifications.

As you can see, universities often make a wide range of career support available for their students (and often their graduates as well). There is a reason for this. It is in the interests of your university for you to be successful and happy in your career choices. All universities report each year on where their graduates have gone six months after their graduation. This survey is called the Destinations of Leavers of Higher Education (DLHE).[xi] DLHE provides a robust source of data on the graduates from all universities. It's how many universities are able to come up with statistics about the number of graduates who are in 'graduate level roles' or in employment. You could argue that six months is not very long for a graduate to get their initial career steps in order, but that is the benchmark set currently for all universities.

The destinations that students from a particular university achieve feed into all kinds of league tables and quality frameworks. These can have an impact on the reputation of your university. So, it really is important to them that you leave university equipped to find meaningful work or study. As a finalist or recent graduate, look out for programmes designed with you in mind – placements, internships, workshops and residentials. There may even be paid internships that only graduates from your university can access. For most universities, career guidance isn't just for recent graduates. You can return as an alumnus to get support and advice as well.

Other university services

Beyond the careers service there are many other student support services available to you. These may not seem to be directly relevant to employment or career decisions, but in fact anything that relates to you and your future will have an impact on your career decisions.

Examples of common student services include:

- welfare and finance advice
- housing advice
- counselling, well being and mental health services
- international student/visa advisors
- legal advice
- disability support.

Depending on your situation and your career plans, you may want to make use of these services. If it feels as if something is getting in the way of you completing your degree or allowing you to focus on making effective career plans, then it might be worth exploring some of these advice services to see if they can help.

Your department or school

Within your academic department or school there will be various sources of support. Your personal tutor will likely act as one of your referees when you make an application. It is a very good idea to work on forming an effective relationship with them. Set up regular appointments throughout your studies if possible. Your personal tutor could have industry connections or ideas about career and study options that you have not yet considered.

TIP: BUILD A RELATIONSHIP WITH YOUR PERSONAL TUTOR

If you are applying for jobs and plan to use your personal tutor as a reference, arrange to go and see them. If you explain the jobs that you are applying for and why you are interested in them it will be much easier for them to write a reference for you.

Within your department there may be alumni events or activities in which you are able to meet with alumni. These can provide new insights into life after university and will expand your networks. Ask your department what information they have about alumni and what opportunities there may be for you to interact with them.

In this book we are focusing on your career and employability at university and afterwards. But we must also remember that studying for your degree is your first and main purpose. Without successfully completing your degree you won't be able to access most of the graduate roles we've been discussing. If your studies start to go wrong, then do make sure that you ask for support from your lecturers, personal tutor and peers. Your department may offer study support or be able to point you in the right direction to access more support for your studies.

Your peers, family and friends

Many of us find work through our existing connections with friends, family and peers. That's why we have devoted all of Chapter 4 to how you can improve your networks and make the most of them.

Make sure that your nearest and dearest know that you are looking for work, and even the type of role or sector you are considering. Your uncle's best friend might be the Chief Operating Officer of the charity you mentioned, or your cousin may have just started a job in the same industry. Make contact with these connections and ask if you can take them for a coffee to talk about their jobs. You might be able to organise a spot of shadowing or even become aware of a job opening.

You should also be calling on your friends and family to support you in the application process. Ask them to check your CV for mistakes, read through your application to make sure you've answered the questions effectively and help you practise for your interviews. Your peers on your course might be going for similar jobs as you, but this shouldn't mean that you feel you are in competition with them. Make use of each other. You will be better off together than you can be on your own.

Work experience connections

The people that you've worked with and for previously can also help. If you've left on good terms (let's hope you have!), then you can contact them and let them know (a) that you are looking for work and (b) that they may be contacted as references.

How can I make the most of this help?

It is easy to say that you should seek out help, but it can be difficult to make that first step. Sometimes we worry that asking for help can make us look weak or expose our vulnerabilities. And that is not something you want to do at a time when you are doing your best to be positive and confident about your skills and abilities!

Consider for a moment how you might feel if a friend contacted you to ask for help. Are you likely to think badly of them or are you more likely to feel valued for the contribution your friend thinks you have to make?

In fact, being able to seek help and support appropriately and effectively shows a great deal of self-awareness and capacity for problem-solving – two attributes that employers recognise and value. Here are some key tips for making sure that you are using the support available to you effectively.

Get connected

There will be services and alerts that you can sign up for. Most careers services will offer an online job shop or some kind of email list that will inform you of new events and presentations in your area of interest. Employers will offer this as well, via social media sites such as LinkedIn, Facebook and Twitter.

There might be student union societies and groups that will offer training, experiences and events.

Your university will send emails to your university account to make you aware of events, presentations and support sessions that it knows might interest you. Open your emails regularly (daily) so that you don't miss out.

Make sure that you have connected yourself to these services so that you are in the know. Don't go mad and sign up for every graduate recruitment site going, but do link to those that are pertinent to you and your situation.

Be prepared

Make sure that you do your research before you ask for help. Have you checked that where you are going is the right service or that the person you are asking is the right person? Have they asked you to complete some information in advance? Career guidance counsellors will often want to know something about you before they meet with you. This is to help them prepare and make the time they spend with you as useful and effective as possible. So take the time to do what you need to do before your meetings.

CASE STUDY

Last week Francis made an appointment to see a career adviser for this afternoon. It's October and he knows he ought to be thinking about making applications for graduate roles. He was told to send his CV in advance and to explain what he was hoping to discuss in the session. But Francis had an essay due this morning and a late night at the union council yesterday, so he hasn't had time to think about the appointment and his CV was in no fit state to share with anyone.

When Francis turns up for his 40-minute appointment the first 20 minutes are spent establishing some basic information about his course, year of graduation, work experience to date and his aims in terms of graduate career – all of which could have been captured in his CV. When asked what he hoped to get out of the meeting Francis realised he wasn't sure and he'd only made the appointment because his final-year lecturer had suggested it in last week's lecture.

The careers advisor was understanding – after all, it wasn't the first time he'd seen an ill-prepared student. He explained that without some basic preparation it was difficult to have a useful and relevant conversation about Francis's career development. The rest of the session was spent exploring some career information and tools on the university website. They agreed that Francis would attend a CV workshop next week and he would return for another appointment to see the adviser the following week.

At the next session Francis was much better prepared. The adviser was able to give him some very useful feedback, make some recommendations for his upcoming applications and suggest two alumni who he knew worked in Francis's field of interest. Francis was pleased with his progress but annoyed at himself that he'd lost three weeks during the peak application period just because he'd not bothered to prepare in the first place.

If you are meeting with a former employer or your personal tutor then prepare for the meeting by giving them some understanding of what you want to discuss. Check that they feel they are the right person to handle your query – this will help to ensure that your time (and theirs!) is well spent.

Part of your preparation should be about reflecting on your experiences to date. Have you had some feedback that you can act on? What have you learned since your last meeting with a careers advisor (for example)?

Be clear

Along with doing research, prepare yourself by thinking about what it is you are hoping to achieve. Are you looking for a sounding board, factual information or a longer discussion about your career aims? If you can be clear about what you are expecting from the service or person you are meeting, then the chances are better that they will be able to help you. Being clear and specific will also help them to think of you the next time they hear about an opportunity or job opening that might suit you. ('Oh look, there's a new role in marketing coming up. Wasn't my personal tutee Kevin interested in marketing? This could be a good entry-level role for him, I'll email him the link.')

Be persistent

People and services can get very busy. And the chances are good that you are seeking out their help at a time when other students are doing the same. So try to be understanding about waiting times and delays in responses. If your personal tutor has not replied to a message within a couple of days, then send her another one reminding her that you are hoping to set up a meeting. You could ask if a telephone call would be more suitable for the time being or if she can suggest a good time to meet.

Be realistic about your expectations. What feels very important to you ('I need to see you about my reference today!') simply may not be a priority for someone else. Try not badger your sources of support, but don't give up either.

Be open and flexible

Be open to events and activities that may not sound as if they are exactly what you are looking for. You might not want to work for a particular employer, but they may be presenting about a sector that you keen to explore. Attend, and listen out for information that could be helpful. Talk to the employer about the sector and industry trends. You may be surprised about what you learn. And even if you don't learn very much, the chances are that it is worth an hour or two of your day to discover that you are already an expert in the field!

Being flexible about your employment aims is a good thing. If you are very rigid in your approach ('I want to work for this company in that location') means that when something you thought you wanted doesn't happen, you feel that you have failed. Commit to your dreams and dream big, but be ready for different types of opportunities and appreciate what they may offer. When you ask people to reflect back on their career paths this is a common story:

> 'I really thought I wanted to go to law school after graduation and become a solicitor. After uni I worked part-time for this company, just to pay the bills. It turns out I loved their ethos and the clients they worked with. It made me think about my priorities. What was I really looking for in a career? When a senior position came up I decided to apply. I've moved on to another company since then but I don't think I would be in this sector now if I hadn't had that first early work experience. I'm so glad I gave it a chance! I really don't think law would have suited me.'

This is a much less common story (though not impossible!)

'After graduation I did exactly as I'd always planned … applied for a graduate position with my favourite bank and got the position I was hoping for in the Midlands office. I started making my way through their trainee programme. Now I've been working in a more senior role in the same organisation for 10 years. I love it! I'm proof that having a career plan and sticking to it does work.'

CASE STUDY

Rachel was planning for a career as an economist. She was hoping to get a role as a civil servant with one of the government departments. In particular she was hoping for a role in the NHS as she liked the idea that her work on trends and data might lead to positive health outcomes for people in the UK. She had been to a presentation about analytical positions in the NHS and was making applications.

Rachel's friend Steve wanted to work for an NGO (non-governmental organisation) and asked Rachel to come along to a careers fair focused on the charity sector. Rachel wasn't interested but Steve didn't want to go on his own, so she decided to attend.

At the fair Rachel got talking to a representative from a major international health charity and discovered that there were research and project roles available there. She'd never considered that she might be able to use her analytical skills for an organisation like that. The more she heard about the opportunity, the more she liked it. The salary was OK, and she'd have the opportunity to travel and make links with similar organisations around the world.

Rachel decided to put applications in to a couple of NGOs and to government analytical departments as well. In the end she decided that a role as civil servant might be something she could do later in life. She accepted a research role with a global health charity and has been to two conferences in Africa already. Steve often reminds her that her success and happiness is all down to him!

Would you like to ... work for an NGO?

Working for a non-governmental organisation can offer you the opportunity to have a career that focuses on making the world a better place. If this appeals to you, then you need to figure out what kind of change you are interested in (environmental, social, political, educational, etc.) and what kind of role you would like to have in an NGO. You could work in marketing, education, outreach, project management, research or fundraising.

There isn't just one way to get a job in an NGO, although internships are quite common in the larger organisations. Work experience, volunteering, speaking an additional language and further study in a specialism are all things that can help you get a job or an internship.

There are a number of places to look for jobs, including the websites for Jobs in NGOs (http://jobsinngos.com), United Nations Careers (https://careers.un.org/lbw/home.aspx?viewtype=SJ&vacancy=All) and Idealist (www.idealist.org).

Return the favour

Take care of your networks and the people who have supported you. Make them aware that you would be happy to help them in the future. You might wonder how you can help an academic or a careers advisor, but don't forget that they need recommendations too. They might think of you the next time they are asked to invite a student to a meeting or event. They may ask you to help another student facing a similar problem, or even invite you back as an alumnus years later to talk to current students about the world of work.

The point is that your relationship with these support services is two way. You don't need to feel obliged to help them and they may never ask for your input, but you are more likely to retain a happy relationship if you nurture your support services.

What about the world wide web?

Google 'Help me with my graduate career' and you will find a ridiculous number of results and resources (over 10 million at our last search). It can be quite difficult to know which ones to use and for what purpose. So below we provide you with examples of what you might want to use and why, with a list of our top five recommended sites. (Many more sites are available!)

Using the web for information

The internet is a great source of information. You might want to find out about career options, recruitment processes or typical salaries in a particular field. As with any information resource, you need to consider the source. Is the site impartial? Is it up to date? Does the information apply to your country or region?

Top five sites

www.prospects.ac.uk – for ideas about what to do with your subject

https://targetjobs.co.uk – for advice and graduate jobs

www.grb.uk.com – for advice and graduate jobs

www.monster.co.uk – for job searches, careers information and uploading your CV for recruiters

www.milkround.com – for job searches and information

Your own university careers website – for information, jobs and opportunities that are open only to students and graduates from your university

Using the web for career tools

You might like to use some career tools to help you to explore career options, to plan your career development or to help prepare you for recruitment activities.

Top five sites

www.prospects.ac.uk/planner – for planning your career development

www.graduatesfirst.com – for free psychometric practice tests

www.myperfectcv.co.uk – for help building your CV (your university will offer free help with this as well) http://myinterviewsimulator.com – for practising interview questions (many universities will also offer interview-recording software that you can use to practise online interviews)

www.icould.com/buzz – for a personality/career quiz and career videos

Using the web for making connections with people and networks

Social media offers us lots of different ways to interact with people. You can connect with people and organisations online in a light-touch way (to keep informed of events and changes in the sector) or in a deeper way (to ask someone to act as your mentor). You can also use bespoke networks to ask questions and seek advice.

Top five sites

www.linkedin.com – for connections to alumni, employers and sectors

www.facebook.com – for connections to peers, alumni, employers and sectors

www.wikijobs.co.uk – for questions about job and for practice aptitude tests

www.thestudentroom.co.uk – for help from your peers about jobs and applications (be wary about lists of interview questions, as employers are also aware of this site and will can change their questions as a result)

www.ratemyplacement.co.uk – for thoughts on jobs and placements from other students, as well as job and placement searches

Don't forget to investigate your own university's online alumni connections. Some even offer online mentoring programmes.

There may not be another time in your life when you are so well supported in seeking work. Everyone wants it to work for you – your academic department, your personal tutor, your careers service, your alumni relations office and, of course, your family and friends. Employers want you to be successful too, that's why they are visiting your campus and spending money and time on you. So make use of it!

IN A NUTSHELL

Hopefully, this chapter has illustrated how many different forms of support there are out there. We hope that as a result you will:

■ recognise when you would benefit from help or support
■ do your research and prepare for meetings and events
■ be open and flexible about where you might find help
■ give help back to others when they need it
■ make use of the many well-crafted online tools and website that are available.

9 THE IMPORTANCE OF PLAN B

Things don't always work out the way you plan. This is nothing to worry about. Plans inevitably have to change, develop and be reimagined as new events come to pass. This is particularly the case for students and new graduates, who typically face a lot of challenges and lucky and unlucky breaks, and who often don't have too much tying them to their original plan. Dealing with these changes, disappointments and unexpected developments is a key skill, but anticipating them is even better.

This chapter will encourage you to plan for the unexpected and get better at reacting positively to the things that surprise you. It will help you to:

- think about the things that can go wrong and consider what you can do about it

- develop a plan B (and C and maybe even D)

- notice how you are changing and think about how this might impact on your plan A

- respond to changes creatively and positively.

Introduction

So far you have been doing a lot of thinking about yourself and what is out there that might interest you. You might also have started to thread your way through the maze of applying for a job or another course. The more time you spend thinking about your career, the more it starts to feel that it is in your control. If you do your research, polish up your CV, prepare for your interview, turn up on time and smile sweetly, surely you are going to get the job.

Well … maybe …

The problem is that there are a lot of other graduates out there as well. Many of them have similar skills and attributes to you, some of them will have been working hard on their career and the lucky few will even have bought this book and know all of the same tricks that we've taught you. This means that even if you are AMAZING, it is possible that there will be other people out there who are just as amazing. They might then get the job of your dreams.

Even if you are sure that you are a SUPERGRAD, ready to conquer all who come up against you, you may still find that things don't work out as you planned. Graduates who finished their studies in 2008 and 2009 weren't expecting that there would be a global economic crisis that would mean that graduate recruitment would go into decline. Sometimes you can spot these changes, e.g. you might be a brilliant political commentator who predicted the Brexit vote and the rise of Donald Trump and adjusted your plan accordingly. But at other times it might be an unexpected wild card; maybe there has been a strike in a nickel mine in the Philippines that has pushed up material costs in the tech industry and led to companies cutting back on recruitment. You never know what might make a difference to your career.

This is why it is important for you to be ready for lots of different possibilities. Yes, things might go as you plan, but more normally there will be at least something that surprises you. If you are ready for this you should be able to manage the change. If you haven't ever thought about what might go wrong you may find that a small gust of wind blows you far off course.

CASE STUDY

Freda has always seen university as a stepping-stone to her real passion of travel. She studied modern languages and specialised in Spanish. During her degree she managed to spend a year at a university in Mexico, which was AWESOME! While she was there she volunteered in a school and taught English.

Once she got back for her final year she started volunteering and teaching English, this time with refugees in the city where she went to university. She also took a third-year module on language teaching and the lecturer helped her to find some language schools in Spain and South America that she could contact. She realises that she might have to do a bit more training, but some of the schools seemed willing to help her to organise that once she got there.

She is just in the process of arranging to fly to Spain for some interviews when she receives some bad news. Her mother has had a bad car crash and is likely to need some pretty intensive support for the next few months. Freda's plan to fly out and start work straight after graduation has to go on hold. Depending on how her mother recovers, she might be able to move in a year or so, but this leaves her stuck. What should she do now? She doesn't have any kind of plan B ...

Would you like to ... teach English overseas?

There are a wide range of routes to teaching English overseas, ranging from some very short courses through to Masters-level qualifications. The variety of routes mean that salary, security and career prospects within this job can vary considerably.

The activity is often referred to as Teaching English as a Foreign Language (TEFL) or Teaching English as a Second Language (TESOL). As global migration increases, along with the number of English speakers, the demand for TEFL teachers looks likely to increase.

It is possible to pursue this career in the UK, but it is often undertaken by those who are keen to travel and work in other countries.

For further information on TEFL teaching view the job profiles on Prospects (www.prospects.ac.uk/job-profiles/english-as-a-foreign-language-teacher) or the National Careers Service (https://nationalcareersservice.direct.gov.uk/job-profiles/efl-teacher).

Preparing to fail or failing to prepare

A good place to start is to think about all of the things that might go wrong. This might seem a bit depressing, but unless you are aware of what is coming your way you can't do anything about what might get in the way of your dreams.

One way to think about this is to view the challenges to your career as a series of concentric rings.

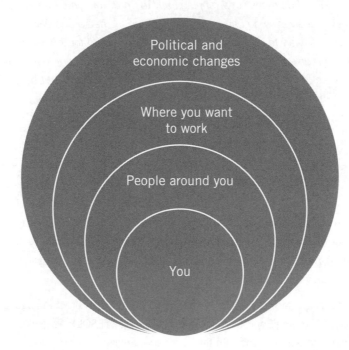

First there are the things that *you* do which might make a difference to your career. For example, you could go out the night before your finals, dance all night and then sleep through your final exam. Or you could get a job that means that you miss all of your Friday lectures throughout the year and then fail a module.

In general you have the most capacity to do something about the things that relate directly to you. However, this isn't always going to be the case in the short term. For example, you may have chosen a course that you now know is too hard or too boring. Ultimately this might have a negative impact on your career, but you can't always do anything about it. Sometimes you just have to deal with these things.

As we move out through these circles you start to have less control. So, if you think about the *people around you*, you may find yourself in a situation where one of your parents becomes ill and looking after them takes away time that you might have spent working on your course or applying for jobs. Or perhaps you are desperately trying to complete an essay in the library when someone sets off the fire alarm and you have to evacuate for two hours. As you move further out and look at *where you want to work*, or even wider, at *political and economic changes*, things get steadily less easy to predict and you have less capacity to affect them.

Thinking in this way can very quickly make you depressed. Are you just an insignificant leaf floating on the ocean, unable to do anything about the direction of your life?

SNAP OUT OF IT!

Of course you can't control everything, but being aware of the challenges does give you a way to do something about it. This process is called 'risk management' and it will be something that you will have to do in most of the jobs that you might do after you graduate – so learning to be a good risk manager is great experience.

Managing the risks in your career

Risk management is a process that you can use to help you to think about and manage the risks associated with any activity. When you make a cup of tea you think about the risks subconsciously and take counter-measures to manage them. For example, you probably take off your roller skates before carrying your cup of tea to your desk! When tasks get more complex you need to become more conscious of the risks that are associated with them.

Many companies require all projects to prepare a list of the risks that are associated with the project (sometimes called a risk register). They may even have a professional risk manager or even a risk management department who lead on this activity.

Would you like to ... become a risk manager?

Risk managers advise organisations on the risks of a variety of projects and activities within the company. They identify and assess threats, put plans in place for if things go wrong and decide how to avoid, reduce or transfer risks.

Risk managers might start on a salary around £20,000 but can earn £70,000 or more as they become more senior. Risk management is a growing area, so it may be worth looking at more as a career option.

For more information on risk management see Prospects, Job Profile: Risk Manager, available from www.prospects.ac.uk/job-profiles/risk-manager. Alternatively, visit the Institute of Risk Management at www.theirm.org.

Of course you don't have to be a professional risk manager to try to do something about some of the risks in your career. There are a few key ideas that you can use to help you to manage risks.

- **Likelihood.** How likely is it that it is going to happen? It is often described as 'high', 'medium' or 'low'. This helps you to make a decision about how far this risk should inform your career planning. It is obviously important to spend more time thinking about how to deal with something that is very likely to happen than with something which is probably not going to happen.
- **Consequence.** What would the result be if this risk did happen? Again, this is often described as high/medium/low. Thinking about the consequence helps you to consider whether you should worry about this at all.
- **Counter-measure.** What can you do to prevent this from happening? Counter-measures set out your strategy to avoid risks.

- **Mitigation.** What could you do, if it did happen, to reduce its impact? Mitigation sets down your thinking about what you can do if things don't go as you hope.

Armed with these tools, you can put together your own risk register for your career. It might look something like this.

Freda's career risks

Risk	Likelihood	Consequence	Counter-measure	Mitigation
I fail my degree	Low	High – I will find it a lot more difficult to find a teaching job without a degree	Work hard to ensure that I get a good degree	Find out more about whether I can re-sit any modules that I fail, or even my final year
No schools are hiring new teachers	Low	High – If this happens I will not be able to pursue my career aspirations	Apply to a range of schools in a range of different countries. It is unlikely that they will all be having the same issues	Explore other jobs that could support my dream of travel (e.g. working in the tourist industry)
My passport is stolen	Medium	Low	Be careful with my passport	Apply for a passport if it gets stolen and inform my prospective employers about the delay
A family member gets ill	Low	Medium to High	Encourage my family to be healthy	Recognise that I may have to change my plans. For example, I could get some experience teaching English in England which would help me to get a job overseas in the future

Consider your risks

Now have a go at building your own career risk register. Think about all of the things that might go wrong and then map out the likelihood and consequence of these things happening. You can then start to plan by developing some counter-measures and building some ideas about how you might mitigate these risks if they do happen.

Setting up some alternatives

Key to managing your risks is starting to set up some alternatives. Establishing plans B, C and D will take you a little bit of time, but it should mean that you are in a much stronger position. Designing your fall-back plan requires you to have a look at your plan A and think about what it is about it that you are really interested in. Once you do that it will usually be easy to work out how you might adapt it to create some other plans.

So, if we take Freda's plan A as an example, Freda wanted to go to Spain or South America to teach English. She was also looking at jobs that included some opportunity to train and maybe even get a qualification. This kind of work appealed to her because it would allow her to travel, to work with people, to develop her career, to use her interest in languages and to help people. Each of these could be turned into a criterion that she ideally wants to see in her plan.

Once she has thought about the criteria that she has used to choose her career she ranks them as follows.

What Freda is looking for in a job

1. Travel
2. Working with people
3. Helping people
4. Using her interest in languages
5. Teaching English
6. In Spain or South America

7. Opportunity to train
8. Opportunity to get a qualification
9. Developing her career

Once she has made this list she realises that there are some things that she would be OK with compromising on. In her case these are largely about her future career development. So this gives her a clear plan B – apply for some jobs that meet most of her other criteria but that don't offer her as many development opportunities.

Ranking her criteria also makes her realise that although she has studied Spanish she is actually not that worried about pursuing her career only in Spanish-speaking countries. So that gives her a plan C – apply for some jobs in other countries.

Finally, she remembers her risk assessment and thinks about what might happen if for any reason she can't travel. She realises that there are actually a lot of other things that are also motivating her. So she decides that plan D should involve her looking for ways to help people and use her language skills while staying in the UK.

It can be helpful to think about your plans on two axes: difficulty and similarity. Difficulty recognises that sometimes it is useful to have a back-up plan in case you are being too ambitious and you can't get into what you want to do. Similarity recognises that sometimes (for a host of reasons) it might be good to have a back-up plan that takes you into a different sector, country or occupation than your plan A.

	Different	Similar
Difficult	Plan C	Plan A
	Something else that excites you perhaps in a different country or sector	Exactly what you want to do
Easy	Plan D	Plan B
	A real fall-back plan Something that you are pretty sure will work out	Pretty much what you want to do but easier to get into, e.g. a lower salary

Creating a series of plans in this way should mean that things can't go too wrong. If plan A doesn't work out you've always got plan B and if this doesn't work out you've still got C and D.

As the Rolling Stones sang '*you can't always get what you want, but if you try sometimes you find you'll get what you need*'. Having multiple plans is about ensuring that you will always get what you need.

It is also important to recognise that failing to get plan A first time doesn't mean that you will never get it. It is very possible to end up doing one of your fall-back plans when you first graduate, but quickly moving back into plan A. For example, you may fail to get onto a graduate scheme and end up doing a non-graduate job (perhaps your plan D). But you may then apply the following year and use your enhanced work experience and increased determination to get back into plan A.

What if they all turn out?

We've advised you to plan multiple futures and to apply for multiple jobs. This is all very well if only one of the plans comes off. But what if you discover that you are hugely desirable and you are being offered job A, B, C and D all at once?

DON'T PANIC! You are not the first person to have to make a choice between different options.

The following are some things to remember when turning down an employer.

1. Employers have seen tens (sometimes hundreds) of graduates before they picked you. It is only reasonable that you should be allowed to go through the same process.
2. A recruitment process allows both the employer and the employee to decide whether the opportunity is a good match to the person. No-one has any interest in recruiting people who don't want to work for them.
3. Employers will have had lots of people turn down offers, fail to show up on the first day and leave after a few hours of work. Be open and honest about what has happened and no-one will blame you.
4. Turning someone down puts you in a position of strength. This is a nice place to be. You might even be able to use it to play one company off

against another, e.g. to increase your salary. But be careful and focus on what it is you really want to do.

5. It's your life!

In short, don't be afraid to turn an opportunity down if you've got a better one. It is also important to remember that your original priorities might not be what you decide to go with. So, by the time that you have some offers on the table it may be that plan C is looking more appealing than plan A.

You will find that different companies' recruitment processes work at different speeds. You may get an offer from one company and accept it, only to get a better one the following month. This is all part of graduate recruitment. If you contact a company and inform it that you have changed your mind, it will find someone else.

In most cases there will be no hard feelings!

TIP: THERE'S NO NEED TO BURN BRIDGES

When you are declining a job offer be professional, honest and tactful. You never know, you might be applying for a job there in a few years' time. The old excuse of 'it's not you, it's me' works just as well with your career as it does when you are dating!

Dealing with failure

It would be nice to think that you will always be in the position of choosing between multiple offers. Careful risk management and the development of alternatives will certainly help to put you in this position. However, we can't promise you that nothing will ever go wrong. Dealing well with failure is one of the most important parts of career management.

Getting yourself into a positive frame of mind

Dealing with failure is all about being positive, optimistic and flexible. You need to believe that things will work out for the best, even if they may not always work out the way that you thought that they would.

When something goes wrong, we'd suggest getting up, putting on some uplifting music and then doing something positive that will drive your career and your life forwards. Things will never get better while you mope around in bed!

TOP FIVE SONGS TO LISTEN TO WHEN THINGS GO WRONG

1. I will survive – Gloria Gaynor
2. All things must pass – George Harrison
3. Been down so long (that it looks like up to me) – The Doors
4. Always look on the bright side of life – Monty Python
5. You can get it if you really want it – Jimmy Cliff

A common problem that many graduates experience is not getting the degree classification that they were hoping for. Many employers will say that they want an upper second class degree (a 2:1). So, if you realise that you are not going to get a degree at that level it may feel like a disaster.

Before you panic you should try to take a step back for a reality check. You may feel that 'all my mates have already got loads of graduate job offers', but this is probably not true. Equally, your fear that 'no-one wants me now I have a 2:2' is also unlikely to be true. Try not to let your emotions run away with you, and focus on the facts.

Recognise that not everything that everyone says in a job advert is an absolute. So an employer may say that they want a 2:1, but they may be quite prepared to compromise on this if they feel that you are the right candidate. It is important not to give up too early.

When something bad happens it is very easy to focus on what it stops you from doing. This doesn't take you very far forwards. In these circumstances it is much more useful to think about what you can do.

But, sometimes you really will fail to get a qualification, job or opportunity that you wanted. The trick is then to try to generate some new opportunities.

Ask yourself what you CAN do, rather than focusing on what you CAN'T do.

- **CAN you just carry on with your original plan?** It is always worth checking that you have actually failed. Maybe you've got so obsessed with getting a first that narrowly missing it has sent you into a downward spiral. But, does your prospective employer even care? It may be that taking a broader perspective helps you to see that you haven't failed after all.
- **What CAN I do with what I've got?** Failing to get a 2:1 or to get admitted onto a graduate scheme might feel as if it is the end of the world. But lots of employers don't care very much about your degree classification and they certainly won't care that another employer has rejected you. It is time to get back on the horse! Resilience will ultimately count for a lot more than any single opportunity.
- **What CAN I do to increase the opportunities available to me?** It is always possible to make yourself more employable. Even if you've failed your degree, you will still have a better chance of finding a job if you are networking, building your work experience, learning new skills and doing all of the other things that we've highlighted in this book. You can only move forwards in life, so it is time to get moving!
- **What CAN I learn from what has happened?** If things have gone wrong you need to think about why this might be. There is no point in dwelling on the past, but at the same time you need to be careful not to keep repeating the same mistakes. Is there anything about what went wrong last time that could trip you up in the future?
- **How CAN I turn this failure to my advantage?** It may seem difficult to imagine, but your current failure may turn out to be the thing that gives you the edge. Think about how you can turn your current situation to your advantage. Maybe failing your degree has given you the wake-up call you finally need to start working hard. Maybe it has given you the chance to rethink what is really important. Maybe the feedback that you were given after interview has finally explained what was going wrong. Re-examine your situation and try to see it from a different angle.

Do you know what failure looks like?

Your future is always unpredictable. Career planning and risk management can help to reduce some of the unpredictability and give you a better chance of finding a career path that works for you, but it will never offer you absolute certainty. Everything may work out perfectly, only for you to discover that your career dream is actually a career nightmare. On the other hand, you may hit a series of barriers and disappointments early in your career, only to discover that things have worked out for the best.

CASE STUDY

Freda spends the first three months after graduation at her mother's bedside, helping to nurse her back to health. As her mother starts to get better she decides to start volunteering again with the refugee support charity that she worked with throughout the final year of her degree.

In this role she can stay close to her mother, but also use her language skills and do some really valuable work. The organisation quickly spots her enthusiasm and skills and offers her a job as a support worker. Freda loves working with the refugees, hearing their stories and helping them to adjust to living in Britain. But she quickly realises that many of them are having a lot of legal problems. This makes her angry and she starts to read up on the law and try to help people.

Six months later, and Freda is passionate about refugee rights and knowledgeable about immigration law. She is keen to play a bigger role in this world and resolves to go back to university to complete the Graduate Diploma in Law and then specialise as an immigration lawyer.

Looking back, Freda realises that she has been on a journey of discovery. If she had followed her original plan to become an English teacher she might never have found the thing that she is really passionate about.

Ultimately you should remember that you can only go forwards in your life and that you can never go back. So the most important question is always to ask where you can go from here, not where you would be if things had worked out differently. You may find out that things turn out for the best and that you are glad that you have ended up somewhere different from where you originally planned.

Would you like to ... work advising people about immigration?

There are a range of ways in which you can help people who are having problems and issues in moving to this country. These jobs range from immigration advisers who might earn around £20,000 per year to barristers who can earn a lot more.

A good place to start is to work with a range of voluntary organisations such as Citizens Advice, Refugee Action or Refugee Support. As you get more experience you may be able to move into paid roles. Legal qualifications can be very useful in this kind of work and open up a range of more specialist and highly paid roles.

For more information on working as an immigration adviser see the National Careers Service, Job profile: Immigration Adviser, available from https://nationalcareersservice.direct.gov.uk/job-profiles/immigration-adviser-(non-government). Alternatively, visit the Immigration Law Practitioners' Association at www.ilpa.org.uk.

IN A NUTSHELL

- Things don't always work out the way that you plan.
- It is important to think about what might go wrong and to try to manage the risks.
- It is very easy to set up some alternative plans. Ultimately this will give you more options.
- All the planning and preparing in the world won't mean that nothing ever goes wrong. But you can be good at dealing with problems and bouncing back.
- When things go wrong, focus on what you can do about it and move forwards positively.

10 STARTING WORK

Congratulations! You've been offered a role and you can now start the next phase of your career! You probably feel relieved and a bit more relaxed than you have done in a little while. The whole 'find a graduate job' process can be quite tiring and relentless. So give yourself a break and celebrate with friends and family. You deserve it.

But don't get too relaxed! Getting a job is only the start of having a successful career, so there will be more to do. In this chapter we will help make the transition to work a bit easier by outlining a number of things you need to consider.

This chapter will help you to:

■ consider your work contract

■ prepare for your first day in your new role

■ make a good impression in the first few days and beyond

■ consider how you will continue your career development in work

■ think about how you leave your first job.

Introduction

After life as a student, going to work can be both liberating and difficult. On the one hand, you have responsibilities and colleagues, independence and a salary! No more essays, lectures or exams (unless you are completing a professional qualification with work, of course). On the other hand, work is sometimes dull and you have to get up and be there on time every day. No more sleeping in, impromptu afternoons in the pub, daytime telly or naps!

Most people feel the trade-off is worth it. It stands to reason that people who engage positively and knowledgeably with work from the very beginning are more likely to enjoy it, be effective and feel happy and successful.

Before you start

You've been made an offer of a job – fantastic. What happens next? There will be quite a few things to consider and do before you start your new job.

Accepting the job

When you get offered a job you will probably receive a verbal offer first, most likely by telephone. You don't have to say yes immediately. If you are happy to say yes immediately, then you can do that too. But it is OK to ask for a day to think about it. It is also fine to say 'YES!' but you should probably also say something like 'I'm really looking forward to starting. Obviously, I'll have to see the formal offer, but in principle count me in!'

Your offer may be 'subject to references'. This simply means that the company has a policy of not offering jobs until all the referees have been contacted and have provided a suitable supporting reference. There is nothing to worry about.

You might receive an email offering you the role. The expectation will be that you will reply to say you want to accept. The employer then has some assurance that you plan to take up the position and they can close down the recruitment. If you have any concerns or questions you can ask them now. Most of your questions will probably be answered in the highly detailed document to come that will be your contract. But it's a good idea to get questions about salary or location nailed down before a contract is issued.

Signing the contract

Your employer-to-be will want to send you a contract to sign. This is rarely left until the day you start your new job. If there is anything in the contract terms that you don't understand, do seek clarification. If you don't want to ask the employer you can take the contract to your careers service for them to look at it with you. Most contracts contain at least some quite formal language and legalese. Try to sift through that to make sure you understand and are happy with what you are signing. You should look out for these details in particular:

- job title/position and responsibilities
- start date
- place of work and hours of work
- salary and any benefits or bonus schemes
- notice period – how much notice do you have to give if you choose to leave (or they ask you to leave)? This would normally be between one and three months
- sick pay. What happens if you are ill?
- holidays.

TIP: WHAT DOES YOUR INSTAGRAM ACCOUNT SAY ABOUT YOU?

Check out your social media outlets (Facebook, Twitter, Instagram, etc.). Would you be 100% happy for your new boss and colleagues to see everything on there? If the answer is yes, then great. If the answer is no, then be sure to change your privacy settings now.

Your first day

You'll want to be well prepared for your first day, and that starts by doing some thinking in advance.

Getting to work

How will you get to work? Do a practice run in advance at the time you will need to travel for a working day. Make sure you have a back-up plan in case your original plan (car/bus/train/bike) doesn't work for some reason. Do you know where you will be able to park or leave your bike? It might seem as if a lot of work to just make sure you arrive on time, but your first impression will be very important. Being late is not an option.

What will you need on day one?

Your employer will likely have provided you with all the information you need to start work. Review your joining instructions or welcome email to check what you have been told. You might need to bring in certain documents on your first day of work (passport, National Insurance number, proof of address, right-to-work documents, visa, etc.). You may be asked to report to Human Resources and/or Security at the beginning of the day to show these documents and get signed in. You might also have to have your photograph taken on your first day so that they can prepare a photo ID or swipe card for you.

Think about what you will do for lunch. If no-one has told you what to expect for lunchtimes, then it is a good idea to bring your own. There might not be many places to purchase lunch. Bring some money as well, though. There may be a chance to go for a coffee or drink at some point in the day and you should be ready to join in.

Bring a notebook and pen. Don't worry too much if you don't remember everything you are told on day one. There will be a lot to take in, with new names, faces, systems and terminology. But give yourself the best chance by using a notebook to write down names and acronyms as you come across them. Do try to make a point to remember the names of the people you will be seated near or walk past each morning. You can also use your notebook to write down questions that occur to you throughout the day.

Don't worry if you don't seem to have much to do on your first day. Your new boss will probably not want to throw work at you until you are settled in. Spend the first few days getting to grips with your place of work and the routine. Serious amounts of work will arrive soon enough!

TIP: MAKE AN OFFICE MAP

Draw a plan of the office in your notebook with the names of all of your colleagues on each desk. This will help you to remember their names and make a positive impression – as well as friends!

Dressing for work

Each work environment has its own 'rules' about what is appropriate work attire. The rules might be spelled out very clearly by the management or they may be simply understood. If this hasn't been made clear to you before you start work, then ask for clarification.

If in doubt, wear what you wore to your interview and observe what your colleagues are wearing when you get to work. You are not likely to go wrong with a smart, professional look but if everyone at work is wearing jeans, then your environment might call for something more casual. Creative work environments and start-up businesses often have a more relaxed approach to office wear. In the finance, accountancy and legal sectors you would normally still expect to see fairly formal attire such as suits for men and women.

In general spend some time thinking about what everyone else is wearing and how they are behaving. A lot of employers are very keen on what is sometimes called 'cultural fit'. This basically just means that they want everyone to fit in and get along. While you shouldn't do anything that will make you uncomfortable, at least start by thinking about what the office culture is, and it should help you to integrate.

Some offices will have 'casual Fridays' or charity days when all staff wear jeans or themed outfits. You will find out about this as you go along and can choose to participate. Make sure 'casual Fridays' don't slip into other days of the week. If you have an important meeting with someone senior on a day that you might normally wear jeans consider whether you want to be casual or not. It is possible the Chief Executive of your company doesn't observe Red Nose day and isn't wearing her spotted onesie to work that day.

Above all, make sure you wear clothes that make you feel confident, comfortable and professional. This will come through in your body language and attitude. Wearing a smile goes a long way as well!

Making a good impression

This is your first job after university and, regardless of whether you want to continue in this company forever or this is just one stop along a varied career journey, you will want to make a good impression. A good impression means a good reference when you leave and that people will think of you first when a new opportunity arises. So here are some pointers to help ensure that your colleagues and boss are happy they chose you.

Be respectful

Be respectful to everyone. Say good morning to all members of staff. Make polite conversation – even when you are not particularly interested in Steve's story of his nephew's birthday party at the weekend. Being respectful and polite will help you to earn everyone's trust and make friends to boot.

Being respectful includes not gossiping about other members of staff. Even if you hear others doing it, try not to join in. You should also be mindful of your language (no swearing) and your humour (no offensive jokes). Of course you should be yourself and bring your own personality to the job, but that shouldn't mean that others feel slighted or side-lined.

Remember that you don't know who is very influential in the company, who is dating the senior manager and whose partner plays basketball with the head of Human Resources. There is no need to get on anyone's bad side, so simply don't do it.

Be reliable

Do what you say you are going to do. If you are asked to complete a task by a particular deadline, then do everything you can to get it done. If it is not possible to get it done it probably isn't because you are not good enough – it's probably because there are unexpected issues. Make your line manager aware of the issues and what you plan to do to get as much as possible of the required work done.

Get in a bit early and stay a bit late. You don't need to spend an extra hour at work every day, but show that you are willing to put in 10 minutes more if a job needs it.

Volunteer to help others out. If you think you can offer some extra time, then do it – just be sure that you can commit before you offer. If there is a new project coming up there might be an opportunity for you to contribute and stretch yourself. If you've built up a track record of being present, committed and reliable, then you are more likely to get the chance to join new initiatives.

Be modest

You might have got the best dissertation mark of your year or received a university prize for your extra-curricular responsibilities, but try not to brag about your achievements. Everyone there will have their own story and their own personal achievements and no-one likes a show-off. It is enough for now for you to know that they chose you for this position. Let your attention to detail, passion and commitment be the way that you show off.

Ask questions

Everyone will expect you to ask questions, so don't feel bad about it. It is much better to ask if you are on the right track with a piece of work than to go too far down the wrong road with it. But think about who you are asking before you ask. Your boss is probably a busy person. She's probably not the right person to ask about the photocopier, for example.

ACTIVITY 10.1

Thinking about your questions

Use your notebook to make a list of questions throughout your first few days of work. Try not to ask these questions as soon as they occur to you.

At the end of each day see which questions you are able to answer just by listening and learning. You may even be able to find out the answers to some by looking them up, e.g. what do tricky acronyms such as FMCG mean (fast-moving consumer goods).

This will probably leave you with a few thorny questions that you can't answer. These are a great set of things to ask your manager or mentor when you have your next meeting with them. Turning up with a list of well thought-out questions will make you look well prepared.

Obviously, if you need to know something desperately, find someone to ask. But you don't want to look as if you just blurt everything out as soon as it comes into your head.

Be prepared and organised

Use your diary effectively that so you know when you have meetings, deadlines, events or key busy periods. Each organisation and industry will run on its own timelines, some of which are set externally (end of financial year, start of academic term) and some of which are set by the organisation itself (monthly reviews, annual conference). Get to know when your busiest periods will be and plan your work accordingly.

Prepare for meetings in the same way you (ought to have) prepared for your lectures. Usually there will be minutes from the previous meeting to read and an agenda for the upcoming meeting. Read through and circle anything you don't understand. Find out what you can prior to the meeting. Are there topics that relate to your area of work? Will you be asked to contribute? Who will be there? Is it normal to bring coffee or tea into the meeting or is this frowned upon?

Be positive, flexible and open

Try to avoid complaining. There will probably be some things that you won't love about work. There might be silly things such as annoying co-workers or a noisy photocopier. Or more significant things such as the pace of the work or the fact that some of the tasks you have to do are just plain boring. Try to avoid complaining or joining in with others who are complaining. If there is a genuine issue it should be raised in private with your line manager.

If you are given a task that is boring try to approach it with a positive attitude and a smile on your face. The chances are that everyone else also has to do boring work some of the time, and there is little to gain from sighing or moaning while you work. Sometimes the boring work is actually the foundations for very important decisions or analysis. Use this opportunity to understand completely what your part in the overall process is. If you are asked to clean a set of data, then consider where it will go next and what impact having clean data has on the company's ability to perform successfully.

Try to present yourself as someone who is open to new ideas and willing to learn new things. This flexibility will mean that you will have the chance to work in different parts of the business, learning more about the different functions and priorities.

Communicate professionally

We've mentioned saying hello, asking questions, being mindful of your language and respecting others. These are all important parts of communicating effectively and professionally. But a great deal of communication at work is done by email. Managing your emails and your inbox in general can be quite tricky. You may find that the volume of emails you receive is an issue and that getting the tone of an email right can be problematic.

You will have written emails as a student. Emails in the workplace may need a bit more thought. Here are a few guiding principles.

1. Use a greeting (Hello, Hi, Good afternoon, etc.) and a sign-off (Kind regards, Thank you, Best wishes, etc.)
2. Use the subject line to make it clear what the topic of the email is.
3. Use full sentences only and avoid text speech.
4. Only write what you would be happy for everyone else to see. If your email contains sensitive (or worse, gossipy) information about another member of staff, then don't send it. It is all too easy to forward an email to another person and something that you never intended to be seen has now been read by everyone in the office, including your boss. Nothing on email can be guaranteed as confidential.
5. You can be still be informal and friendly in your emails. Professional doesn't have to mean that you are overly formal or robotic. Be yourself, but the best version of yourself.
6. Don't click 'Reply All' when replying to a message unless you really think that everyone needs to hear your answer. The same goes for using group email lists.
7. As a general rule don't use the Bcc function. Bcc stands for 'Blind carbon copy'. If you send an email to someone you can send the same email to someone else at the same time without the other recipients knowing. A good use of Bcc is when you want to send a message to many people but you want to keep their names and email addresses confidential from each other.
8. Proof-read and double check that you are sending the email to the correct recipients before clicking send.
9. If you are really struggling to write an email it might be because you ought to be talking to the person face to face or by telephone instead.
10. Use normal font and avoid using underline, bold and italics. CAPITALS CAN GIVE THE IMPRESSION THAT YOU ARE SHOUTING AT THE RECIPIENT. If you need to make something very clear or important you can do this by writing your concerns simply, possibly in a short list of bullet points. An overly long email probably means that you should be having a conversation or writing a document to outline your instructions or key points.

TIP: KEEP ON TOP OF EMAILS

Manage your email inbox by using folders to file emails according to their subject or business function. This will help you to reduce the number of emails sitting in your inbox on an ongoing basis and can help you to be (and feel) more organised.

Another point to remember about professional communication is body language. This will be most obvious when you are in meetings. Take note of how others behave. The people who are most respected and listened to are probably showing their interest in the topic with their body language. Be sure to sit up, face towards the meeting and make eye contact with those who are speaking.

CASE STUDY

Amanda started at a large media company three weeks ago as a project officer. It was really exciting starting work but she is finding it a rather big change from her life as a student! No more naps or daytime telly. Getting up at 7:00 every morning to get to work on time is not easy. But Amanda is keen to succeed in this role. She knows that with a bit of effort this job will lead to more interesting work, fantastic connections and the senior editor position she dreams of.

Amanda's line manager, Kerry, is impressed with her so far. Kerry has noticed that although Amanda's hours are 9:00–5:00, she is always in work a few minutes before 9:00 and stays a bit later than 5:00. This simple thing has left a much different impression than last year's intern, Charlie. Charlie almost always arrived five or ten minutes late and made sure he was packed up and ready to leave the office at 4:59 each day. The quality of his work was fine but he never put himself forward for extra projects and it never really felt like he wanted to be there.

Stay focused on work

There can be a lot of distractions in the workplace. Some of these are positive and can help you to build relationships and learn (coffee breaks, sharing plans for the weekend). Others can be less helpful (catching up on celebrity gossip online, posting to your uni friends whatsapp group). What might make it difficult for you to concentrate? What can you do about it?

Be prepared not to look at your phone or social media during working hours. The best policy is to keep your phone in your bag or desk drawer and not get it out unless there is a call or you are having a lunch break. You will probably see other people in the office looking at their phones as and when they feel the need. There will probably come a time when you will feel comfortable doing this as well, but first you need to demonstrate that you can be trusted to stay on task and not get distracted. The best way to do this is to simply put the phone away.

This goes for social media on your computer at work as well. Unless your job is in media or communications there is unlikely to be an urgent need for you to have Facebook or other non-work sites open on your computer. You might only check once or twice, but if you are caught by someone else then the impression will be that you have time to waste at work.

TIP: PUT YOUR PHONE AWAY

Put your phone on silent/vibrate and let friends and family know that they can't expect an immediate reply from you while you are at work. Give key people your work telephone number so that you are contactable if there is a genuine need. You can then leave your phone in your bag or desk drawer knowing that you might miss a few text messages, but nothing that can't wait until lunchtime or after work.

Office politics

The office world is a microcosm of the real world. There are people with all sorts of different backgrounds, personalities, cultures and agendas. Understanding who is who can be quite a difficult task. So go carefully. Keep to your principles of respecting and including everyone, and you can't go wrong.

It will start to become clear who the decision-makers are and who is very influential in the running of the organisation. Sometimes a strong personality and years of experience can mean that someone who is less senior than you will have more authority than you and your line manager.

It is also worth getting to understand what your different business functions are up to. The overall business will have a strategy and each business function will have a role to play in that. Let's say you work in marketing and your role is to ensure that the brand and products of the company are well recognised in your target market. John works in finance and he is all about making sure that the different business functions stick to their budgets. These two aims may not be compatible, as you have decided you need to spend £30,000 on an upcoming advertising campaign. So there can be tensions between one part of an organisation and another, even though their overall aim should be shared.

TIP: LEARN ABOUT BUSINESS TARGETS

One way to better understand the aims of each business function is to find out what their performance measures are. They likely have targets (e.g. 'keep budgets to within 1% of predicted spend' or 'increase sales by 5% by 2020'). These targets will probably reveal a lot about their motivations and actions. What are the measures for your business function?

CASE STUDY

Connor has landed a great job in a consultancy firm. He is enjoying the job and the people. One of the things he likes best so far is that he is learning something new all the time.

Some of the work he has been given is a bit junior and boring – fact checking, report summaries and data cleansing. But this also means that Connor gets access to some high-level management documents. He has read the latest company reports and the soon-to-be-published strategic plan. As a result, he has a much-improved understanding of the organisation's targets and where they expect business to grow (as well as where it may not).

Connor is making sure to keep his ears and eyes open. What he has learned so far makes him think there will be some new investment in staffing in his division, which could mean a development opportunity.

Would you like to ... work in consulting?

Consultancy is one of the most popular graduate careers. Consultancy is about helping organisations to solve the problems that they have. Typically this focuses mostly on business strategy, management, organisation, operational processes and technology. You may feel that you don't have enough experience to start offering other people advice, but consultancy companies will take bright graduates and train them up. Initially you will probably work as the junior member of the team, doing research and supporting the lead consultant. As you develop you will be taking an increasingly leading role.

There are a wide range of different kinds of consultancy jobs, but the most common are found in large professional services companies or specialist consultancies. Competition for these roles is usually pretty fierce, but they are also big recruiters of graduates. Your careers service will be able to advise you about the best way to get these roles.

Salaries often start around £25,000–£30,000 but can go up pretty quickly in the right companies. Consultancies recruit from a wide range of degree subjects, but typically value candidates who have good numeracy and analytical skills.

For more information see the Prospects jobs profile (www.prospects.ac.uk/job-profiles/management-consultant) or have a look at specialist sites such as Consultancy UK (www.consultancy.uk).

Making friends

It can be hard to make friends in a new office. If you are lucky you will be starting with a few other graduates and then you will have an instant support network. But it might also be that you are the only person starting that month, or perhaps even their first graduate recruit. You will be spending a significant portion of your life at work, so making some friends is actually very important not just for your ongoing career but for your health, happiness and well-being.

Be social

We've already mentioned being friendly and respectful, so you will be off to a good start. You can also try finding out if there are work socials, groups or outings that you can join in on. Perhaps there is a group who go walking at lunchtime, or a few who like to go to the cinema once a month. If there aren't any of these things then you can make a suggestion – who fancies the new *Star Wars* film at the end of the week?

If there is a tradition of going to the pub on a Friday after work (for example), do try to join in. You don't have to drink alcohol, and in fact it probably isn't a good idea to drink too much. Our judgement and reason is quite quickly affected by alcohol and you could easily spend the weekend regretting the conversation about your favourite YouTuber that you had with your boss.

Give to others

Friendship is built on reciprocity. Show an interest in others' lives and concerns. Listen and contribute to office conversations. You can give your time to a colleague for a work project or offer help to a colleague who is moving house. Your offer of help may not always be taken up but it will be appreciated and remembered.

Bringing in homemade biscuits or a box of chocolates is also welcome in most offices and is another way that you can give to your colleagues.

Be yourself

A lot of what we have been suggesting may sound as if we are proposing that you pretend to be someone else at work. But this isn't at all the case. You should feel comfortable showing who you are and what your likes and interests are. If you have your own desk space, bring in photos or other memorabilia that show where some of your key passions lie. Colleagues will ask why you have a mug with a horse on it and you'll have the chance to tell them all about your horse-riding hobby.

Continuing your career development

We've stated several times in this book that career management is a lifelong skill and that excellent career development means calling on this skill over and over again at different points in your life/career. So clearly we wouldn't expect you to leave your career management skills at the door of your new company.

Hopefully you have chosen a company that sees value in professional and personal development as well. Most medium to large organisations have staff development support, formal processes for reviewing your progress and opportunities for further training. These will all play an important part of your career plan.

Review your progress

You may have a probation period as part of your initial contract. A probation period is a fixed period of time during which your employer is assessing your suitability to the role. It might be three months, six months or possibly a year. At the end of the period you might be issued a new contract or simply informed that you have passed your probationary period. It is nothing to worry about, but it is important that you are aware and follow the company protocols.

Your organisation will probably have a formal review process as part of your probation period. So there will probably be meetings where you set some objectives, review your objectives and make plans for how your objectives might be better met. These might be called professional development review (PDR) meetings or something similar. Your objectives will likely be set out in SMART targets (Specific, Measurable, Achievable, Relevant and Time bound), which will help them to be clear and easier to measure.

TIP: MAKE USE OF A MENTOR

Seek out a mentor. This should be someone more senior and experienced than you who is not your line manager. They don't have to be in exactly the same job function as you but you would need to be clear about the benefit you are hoping to gain from this. You can ask your line manager for a recommendation. A mentor can guide you through workplace politics, help you to recognise opportunities for development and link you up with other key contacts.

In addition to a formal review process you will likely have weekly or regular catch-up meetings with your line manager or supervisor. These are opportunities for you to seek feedback on your day-to-day work and duties. You might also check on the progress you are making towards your agreed objectives in these meetings. Be sure to ask for feedback regularly as part of these meetings. It can be as simple as saying, 'I know I've been here four weeks now, do you have any concerns about any areas of my work?' These meetings will probably be less formal, so there won't be a written record of your conversations and progress. You can make notes for your own professional development.

Out of these formal and informal reviews you or your line manager may identify some training or areas for development.

Set your own goals

Outside of the formal and informal reviews of your professional work you should consider what your own goals are. Depending on the nature of your goals you may want to share these with your line manager. Certainly if you are looking to stay within the same organisation and progress, then it would be of benefit to make your line manager aware that this is your intention. Likewise, if you feel that you are enjoying the company but you think you'd prefer to move to a different role or business function you should share this with your line manager. He may be in a position to help you get the experience you need to make this type of move, or perhaps to offer you the chance to do some shadowing in another part of the company.

If you've come to the conclusion that you would like to make a change in industry or organisation then you might want to keep this to yourself for now.

Whatever your goals, it will be easier to review and notice your progress if you make them SMART.

Leaving your first job

It might seem crazy to talk about leaving when you have only just started! And it may be that you stay at this company for many years to come. Your colleagues will become like family members and you will come to know the industry and company inside and out.

But perhaps you've put all of our advice and guidance to good use and you've made such a great impression that you've been head-hunted for the competition! Or perhaps you've been reflecting on your skills, values and experience and decided to take your career in a different direction in a new opportunity. If this is the case, then congratulations are in order and let's talk about how you leave your current role.

Are you sure?

Be sure about what you want to do. Your current company might make a counter offer. Is that something you would consider? If so, what terms are you seeking? More money? Different role? Additional responsibilities? Be clear about your goals before you talk with your line manager.

Giving notice

Before you speak with your line manager, check what your notice period is. This will normally be one to three months. You can then propose an end date to your contract.

This conversation with your line manager is best done face to face (or by telephone if necessary). Make an appointment to see her and explain where you are in terms of the new job. Let her know how much you appreciate all the support and development you have received and how much you have enjoyed working for the company.

You can discuss your new role briefly and then try to come to an agreement about your end date. You can also talk about producing handover materials so that the person coming into your role will have information about how to proceed in your absence. There may be key deadlines coming up and it will be helpful if you have thought about how these activities will be completed if you are not there to assist with them.

Starting over in your new company

The important thing about leaving your current job is to make sure you leave on excellent terms. You don't know when you might want to return to this company. And the organisation may have a big influence on the industry as a whole, which means you are likely to run into colleagues again if you plan to work in the same industry. For this reason you should be careful not to rubbish your old company or colleagues when you get to your new role. The world that you work in is usually much smaller than you realise!

Although you will be starting over in a new organisation, it won't be the same as starting your first graduate job. Even if you are starting a brand new role in a completely different sector or industry you will have lots of transferable skills, knowledge and experience to take with you. You can continue to use the principles in this book to help you make the most of your career in your new role, but you will also have the experience of your first transition to reflect on and learn from.

IN A NUTSHELL

Starting work is stressful and exciting! To be at your best you will need to:

- consider what you need to do before you start work
- plan for your first day
- make a good impression on your colleagues and senior staff
- get to grips with the office politics
- be sociable and making friends
- make an action plan for your continuing development
- know when it is time to leave and leave on good terms.

11 IF AT FIRST YOU DON'T SUCCEED ...

Sometimes jobs aren't what you expect. Other times, graduates may find themselves in jobs that they never wanted in the first place. In this chapter we discuss how you can make the best of situations that are not everything that you hoped for and use them to your advantage.

This chapter will help you to:

■ deal with setbacks

■ turn the job that you have into the job that you want

■ decide when you should stick with a job and when you should move on

■ explain how to make the most of the experience that you are gaining.

Introduction

When you went to university you probably thought that getting a job at the end of it was going to be pretty straightforward. Once you were armed with a degree, employers should have been knocking down your door. Unfortunately, as we've shown in this book, it isn't always as simple as that. There are a lot of graduates and not so many 'graduate jobs', so it is quite possible that you are going to find it difficult to get the kind of job you were hoping for.

In this chapter we are going to talk about how to deal with this kind of disappointment and turn your situation around. But the most important thing to remember is that the job that you get straight out of university is not going to determine the rest of your life. This is just the first step on your journey, and so there is still plenty of time for you to change, develop and re-orientate you career. It is also worth noting that we can't always spot opportunities as soon as we see them, and so you may find that what you currently feel is a huge failure turns around over the next few months. There is a lot to be said for a positive attitude.

I'm just doing nothing …

When should you get a job after you finish your degree? Ideally you would have applied for a graduate scheme, but you didn't, and so once exam time comes around you just focus on doing really well in your exams. Then, once you've done your exams you are relaxing a bit, but also waiting for your results. Then, when your results come it is only a couple of weeks until graduation.

So you walk across a stage and get presented with your degree and then go to the graduation ball. At the ball you learn that lots of your friends have already secured some pretty exciting job opportunities. You're pleased for them, but you are already starting to feel like a bit of a failure in comparison. The next week you clear out your student house and head back to your parents. They invite you to join the family holiday and you go off and catch a few rays of sun. When you get back you catch up with some old school friends and then start thinking about jobs. What should you do next?

The problem is that all of these perfectly reasonable activities have taken you months since you finished your degree. You are now skint, unemployed and living with your parents. This wasn't how it was supposed to go ...

If you do find yourself unemployed after graduation you shouldn't panic. It has happened to generations of students before you. No-one will be surprised if you have a gap of a couple of months on your CV after graduating. But you also need to get focused, because you don't want it to turn into six months or a year.

ACTIVITY 11.1

Why are you where you are?

If you are unemployed it is worth spending a little bit of time thinking about why you have ended up in this situation. Common reasons include the following.

- I just never thought about getting a job while I was at university.
- I never got round to putting in any applications.
- I lack confidence and I thought that no-one would ever want me so I avoided putting in any applications.
- I put in loads of applications, but none of them worked out.
- I am waiting for my dream job to come along.

Once you've thought about the reason why you are where you are it will usually become much clearer what you should do next.

Now ask yourself these questions.

- What have I learned about myself?
- What have I learned about the labour market?
- What should I do next?

For example ...

Why am I unemployed?	What have I learned about myself?	What have you learned about the labour market?	What should I do next?
I applied for loads of jobs with accountancy firms but I didn't get any of them.	That I'm focused and have a good idea about what I want to do.	That getting into accountancy is competitive.	Get some help to find out why none of my applications has been successful.
			Keep applying, maybe trying some smaller companies. I also might widen my search to other kinds of graduate jobs.

Step one: get some benefits

Depending on how imminently you think that you might be able to get a job, you might want to investigate whether you can access some benefits.

TIP: FIND OUT ABOUT BENEFITS

The government provides some information about claiming benefits at www.gov.uk/jobseekers-allowance/eligibility. This includes a useful benefits calculator that may be helpful to you in understanding what you will be able to get.

There is nothing to be ashamed of in signing on for some benefits. Depending on your situation you may need them to eat or pay the rent. You may also find that once you start applying for jobs and getting interviews you need a bit of money to pay for travel and so on. In addition, you may find that once you have signed on you can access some help with your CV and job searching.

Step two: get some help

The next step is to get some help. If you haven't applied for any jobs so far, you probably need a bit of help getting you started. If you have applied for a bunch of jobs but haven't got any of them you really need to talk to someone to try to work out why this is the case.

It is always a good idea to draw in help from as many people as you can. We've already covered sources of support in Chapter 8. We'd suggest that you re-read that and think about who can help you now.

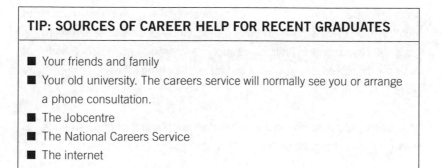

TIP: SOURCES OF CAREER HELP FOR RECENT GRADUATES

- Your friends and family
- Your old university. The careers service will normally see you or arrange a phone consultation.
- The Jobcentre
- The National Careers Service
- The internet

Your university will offer a range of help and support, specifically for people in your situation. It is important to your university that you are able to access work or further study. Your success reflects well on it, so there is often a great deal of support available to graduates who have just completed their degree and haven't quite managed to get a graduate-level job. Support that your university is likely to offer includes the following.

- **Internship programmes that are open only to graduates from your university** (this reduces the competition for these roles drastically!) These roles are often fantastic projects with smaller local or regional companies and they can lead to a permanent job. Even if you are not after a permanent job in that part of the country, do consider giving these jobs a chance. A six-month temporary move could put you into a completely different situation in terms of work experience and contacts.
- **Free career guidance, workshops or even residentials** designed specifically with recent graduates in mind. These sessions will sometimes involve employers directly, so you can get access to the types of people who are still looking to employ a graduate.
- **Funding for you to start your own business.** Enterprise and entrepreneurship is getting more and more support from universities and through

government-funded initiatives. Your university may have funding that you can bid for to help you start up your own company.

So, your first call for help should really be to your own university careers service to find out what it has to offer you to help ensure your success.

Step three: apply for a job

Getting a job starts with putting in an application. If you are sitting around with nothing to do there is no reason why you shouldn't be able to devote pretty much all of your time to finding and applying for work. In Chapters 5 and 7 we have discussed the process of finding and applying for work, so you might want to re-read these.

In essence, finding a job requires a lot of research and a lot of persistence. Thankfully, you have the time for both now.

TIP: IF YOU STILL DON'T KNOW WHAT YOU WANT TO DO JUST APPLY FOR ANYTHING

In previous chapters we've encouraged you to spend a lot of time thinking, researching, reflecting and exploring what it is that you want to do. If you haven't done any of this yet, then now is the time! But if you still don't know you might be better to just do something. If you take a job you might like it – in which case great, you've lucked out! Alternatively, you might hate it, in which case you will know what it is that you don't want to do. Sometimes experience is the best teacher, and so now is a good time to take a chance on something new.

Step four: Get experience and get networking

If you are unemployed or under-employed you can still be building your employability by getting experience and networking with people in the field that you are interested in. We've talked about this in Chapters 3 and 4 and so you might want to revisit these.

Key activities that you could be doing as a new graduate include:

- volunteering with organisations that interest you
- contacting professionals in the field you are interested in and asking if you can shadow them or speak to them
- going to meetings of professional associations and sector bodies
- finding out what your other recently graduated friends are doing and exploring whether there are any jobs in their companies.

Step five: get a job, any job

One of the key dilemmas that new and unemployed graduates have is whether they should apply for a job that they don't want.

Our advice is generally – yes! Any job is better than being unemployed!

A reasonable concern with this is that if you start working you may find that you have less chance to research and apply for jobs that really interest you. Depending on your financial situation and the willingness of your parents to support you, it is reasonable to give yourself a period of time to research careers, gain some voluntary experience and put in some applications. However, if you are going to do this be really honest with yourself about whether you are making the most of this opportunity. If you've spent a weekday playing Xbox you really need to get a job. You should also set a time limit for how long you want to be unemployed. Three months of unemployment after graduation is nothing unusual, but six months is starting to look like a pattern.

In general, getting a job, any job, is usually a good move. Working will get you into a routine, teach you some employability skills and open up some opportunities and networks that you might not expect. Even more importantly, it will give you some money!

Even if you are going for a job that you aren't that excited about you should still treat the application and interview seriously. No-one will employ you if you tell them that you don't really want the job. You might think that you are *too good* to flip burgers but the manager of Crabby Patty will only be interested in whether they think that you are *good enough*. You need to be able to convince any employer that you are competent and that you have a good attitude.

If you are going to go for a stop-gap job there are a few things to think about that might turn it into a career opportunity.

- **Good pay.** I'm sure that we don't have to tell you this, but finding a better-paid job will make your life easier and also help you to negotiate a better starting salary in your next job.
- **Flexibility.** If you are keen to move on quickly to another job you might have to go to interviews fairly often. You want to find a job that will allow you to do this.
- **Related to your interest.** Finding a job that relates to your interests can be a really good way to get into an industry. If you get a job as a receptionist or assistant in a company that you want to work for, you will get the chance to meet key staff and tell them that you are really looking to move up fast.
- **Learning opportunity.** Some jobs might give you a chance to learn some new skills or knowledge that may be useful for your future career. Taking advantage of these kinds of learning opportunities will really pay off for your career in the long run.

Step six: get the job you want

If you seek help, get some experience, build your network, apply for jobs and treat any interim jobs as an opportunity you will find that you will very quickly be able to move towards the job that you want.

Under-employment and disappointing destinations

A lot of graduates find that they end up in jobs that are less interesting and less well-paid than they feel that they deserve. Unfortunately there is no law that states that every graduate should get a great job, and in fact the supply of graduates is far greater than the number of graduate jobs that are out there.[xii]

The graduate labour market is changing all the time and it can be difficult to keep up. The jobs and skills that graduate employers are looking for are always changing (although there is also a core set of skills that people are interested in). It isn't essential that you become a labour market analyst, but keeping your eye on the trends in the graduate labour market can be useful. Some good sources of information include the following.

- Association of Graduate Recruiters (www.agr.org.uk)
- Government graduate labour market statistics (www.gov.uk/government/collections/graduate-labour-market-quarterly-statistics)
- HECSU – Graduate market trends (www.hecsu.ac.uk/current_projects_graduate_market_trends.htm)
- HECSU – What do graduates do? (www.hecsu.ac.uk/current_projects_what_do_graduates_do.htm)
- High Fliers Research (www.highfliers.co.uk)

TIP: UNDERSTANDING THE DIFFERENCE BETWEEN A GRADUATE AND A NON-GRADUATE JOB

There are a range of jobs that have traditionally been filled by graduates, such as teachers, lawyers, doctors, bankers, civil servants and so on. However, the graduate labour market has got a lot more complicated and the number of graduates has grown. This means that it can now be difficult to make a clear distinction between what is a graduate job and what is a non-graduate job. For example, how would you classify a job which 10 years ago was done by school leavers (and so presumably doesn't *require* a degree) but which now is almost universally filled by graduates?

Researchers at the University of Warwick have argued that these days graduate jobs tend to fall into one of three categories.[xiii]

Experts. Jobs that require degree-level knowledge and skills. Examples include chemical scientists, civil engineers, pharmacists, solicitors, physiotherapists, chartered surveyors and airline pilots.

Orchestrators. Jobs that require you both to draw on your knowledge and to make intelligent use of the knowledge and skills of others. Examples include managers, coordinators and directors of various kinds.

Communicators. Jobs that require interactive skills that may be based on interpersonal skills, creative skills or high-level technological knowledge, capacity to access and manipulate information and/or an understanding of how to communicate information effectively to achieve objectives. Examples include journalists, actors, conference and exhibition organisers, web-design and -development professionals and marketing associate professionals.

There are a few reasons why you may feel that your job is not 'graduate enough' and that you could do better.

- You are doing a job where most of the people around you aren't graduates and/or the skills required to do the job do not make any use of the skills or knowledge that you developed at university.
- You are doing a job which is at graduate level but which is very badly paid.
- You are doing a job which is at graduate level, and which is paid OK, but your employer is able to offer you only part-time employment.

All of these situations are different kinds of under-employment. This doesn't mean that all of these jobs are bad jobs, that you will not learn anything through doing them, nor that they will necessarily hurt your career prospects. However, it is reasonable to start to develop a strategy to move your career on past your current job.

CASE STUDY

Latitia graduated in July and needed some money desperately. So she quickly applied for a job in a pub where she had worked as a student. They were pleased to have her back, but she knows that she doesn't want to work pulling pints for long. She is really looking to move into the marketing field, as this was one of the bits of her business studies degree that she enjoyed most.

She starts working and makes an effort to do a really good job. Because she is mainly working in the evenings she has her days free to research career options and apply for graduate schemes. She realises that there are actually loads of opportunities still out there, even though she has left it a bit late.

She also spends some time talking to her managers at work. She discovers that they started on a graduate scheme and that the pub where she works is part of a big hospitality chain. Her managers tell her that when they were training they got to spend some time in all of the main business functions in the chain (including marketing).

She uses her inside knowledge of the business and her work experience to make an application for this scheme and quickly gets an interview. When she turns up for the interview she is told that every year a few students drop out and new places open up on the graduate scheme late in the summer. After an interview and a day at an assessment centre she gets a call.

'Can you start in September?'

A key part of any strategy for career development is doing the job that you are doing well. You will be relying on your current managers and colleagues for a whole host of things. Your working relationships are going to have a big influence on your happiness. If everyone thinks that you are great at your job, everything is going to be a lot more fun than if you are known as the miserable one who is always moaning that he is too good for this place.

Would you like to ... work in hospitality?

Very few graduates dream of working in a bar or waiting tables. But the hospitality industry is an enormous sector with a huge number of job opportunities. As well as obvious roles such as managing bars and restaurants there are also a range of more specialist roles such as chefs or sommeliers. You could also find yourself working in almost any job within this sector. You'll find everything from accountants to web designers working in the field. You'll even find roles such as lobbying and political analysis in this (and pretty much any other) sector.

As with most sectors, knowledge about what the sector does and how it works is critical. So you may yet be able to put your experience working as a waitress in a cocktail bar while you were a student to work! One of the most exciting things about this sector is that it may afford you the opportunity to travel – perhaps your next job could be as a hotel night manager in Switzerland or the entertainment manager on a cruise ship!

There are lots of different routes into a career in the hospitality industry, but getting onto a graduate scheme at one of the bigger hospitality chains is a pretty good start. Your university careers service should be

209

able to help you to access these schemes. However, most jobs boards will advertise hospitality jobs of all levels. There are also some specialist sites, such as the Hospitality Guild (www.hospitalityguild.co.uk), and jobs boards, such as Caterer.com (www.caterer.com), which you might find particularly useful if you are interested in this sector.

Your manager will also be one of your references for any future jobs that you go for. If she thinks (and is willing to write in your reference) that you are hard working, good fun to be around, liked by customers and capable, it will really help you to get your next job. If she spends a lot of time telling you to stop daydreaming or messing around, or you are repeatedly late for work, looking at your phone mid-shift or pulling sickies, then your reference might not be so great.

TIP: CHOOSE YOUR REFEREE NOW

You will have to use your current employer as a reference for most jobs that you go for. Make sure that the reference is going to be a good one. You will often be able to pick the manager with whom you get on best and you should let them know that you are going to use them as a reference before they get approached by your prospective employer.

Finally, it is always worth noting that a great career can emerge from the unlikeliest of places. In bigger firms you may be able to use a non-graduate job as a way of doing your research and getting onto a graduate scheme. In smaller firms you may be able to develop your job, gradually build it up and turn it into a graduate job. This technique is called '*job crafting*' and it is one of the most common ways that people develop their career. Usually you find that you get the responsibilities before you get a new job title or any more money, but spotting opportunities and taking on more responsibility will enhance your employability and increase your leverage to ask for a pay rise. It will also mean that when a role with more responsibilities and better pay comes up in another organisation, you will have improved your chances of getting the job by being able to show that you are already experienced.

Don't get distracted, don't give up

If you are working in a non-graduate job it can be very easy to settle into it. If you work with nice people and the work is interesting or fun you can go from day to day, week to week and so on without thinking about your future. You are now getting paid and you are tired at the end of the day, so applying for any future jobs can seem less urgent.

If you find yourself in this situation the key thing is to think about whether you will really be happy if you work in your current job for a long time. If the answer is no, you need to do something about it. This means devoting some of your precious non-work time to your career. We think that if you spend an hour a day developing your career by focusing on some of the things that we have talked about in this book you'll see results pretty quickly. This means that you need to get up an hour earlier or spend an hour in the evening researching jobs, networking online or putting in applications. This will require a lot of discipline, but it won't be forever, and it will be worth it.

I've got a graduate job, but it isn't what I thought that it would be

Another common problem that graduates face is that the (graduate) job that they have got is not really what they thought it would be. Maybe you've got a job as an economist for a big bank. You thought that you'd be steering the global economy, but you are actually just sitting in a cubicle checking someone more senior's spreadsheets all day. Or perhaps you have landed a job as a research scientist, but instead of making scientific breakthroughs you are just pipetting colourless liquids from one place to another.

This sucks …

The good and bad news is that being disappointed, confused, out of your depth, frightened, lonely and depressed is incredibly normal in your first job. You are making a major life transition from student to worker and you should expect this to be difficult. So, before you make any big decisions think about what might be happening.

What is happening to you	Why it is happening	What you can do about it
You've been in the job for a few months and you spend all of your time getting low-level and boring work.	The company is testing you out and using you to do some of the basic stuff.	Show that you are competent, reliable and have a good attitude and you will gradually get better work. This time next year someone else will be the new recruit. Remember that your contribution is part of a bigger process – use your work to build your understanding of the business.
Nobody speaks to you apart from to dump new bits of work on you.	A company is a busy place. Everyone else already knows each other. They may even feel a bit shy coming up to you.	Try to put yourself in situations where you will meet people through work (e.g. volunteer for projects or to attend meetings) or around work (e.g. accept the invitation to Friday-night drinks or to play in the office football team).
You can't do the work that you are given.	Your boss and your colleagues don't know what you are capable of and they are getting it wrong.	See if you can learn how to do the work by yourself (e.g. buy a book and spend your evening learning that new bit of software). Everyone will be impressed if they see you develop. If you can't figure it out, speak to your manager and ask for some training and support.
You're expected to work all hours of the day and night.	Some companies have fairly unhealthy attitudes to work–life balance. Unfortunately this is often particularly the case for junior staff.	Work out who is working ridiculous hours. Is it (a) just you (b) just people at your level or (c) everyone in the company? If you are not happy with the work–life balance that this company offers you, you might want to talk with your line manager or start preparing your exit strategy.

You've realised that you aren't interested in this company, sector or type of work.	It is often difficult to anticipate what we will like and dislike before we have done it. Now you have experience, you have more information.	Think about what aspects of your job you do like. Is there any way that you can job-craft to make your job focus on these aspects?
		Thinking about what you like and don't like in your current job will also help you to think about what alternative jobs you might enjoy more.

In general, transition into a new role requires a lot of resilience. You should expect that things will be difficult and resolve to keep going even though there are some challenges. However, you shouldn't be unhappy all the time for a long while. If things aren't going well, talk to other people and then do something about it. You can change the way you fit into your workplace, influence how your boss and colleagues treat you and ultimately move on.

You have more power than you think!

When is the right time to move?

Once you've found a job you may start thinking about your next career move. You are likely to think about this a lot quicker if you are unhappy, but however your current job is going you should probably keep one eye on the future. But when is it OK to move? And what will employers think if you move on too quickly?

The first thing to say is that it is very common for graduates to move on quickly. In fact this is something that worries graduate employers and is likely to make them try to convince you to stay.[xiv] No-one will think anything of it if you quit one job to move on to another one. Early on in your career most people expect you to shop around a bit. However, if you are repeatedly quitting your job and spending periods unemployed this might start to raise some questions. No-one wants to employ a hot-head who is always storming out.

The key thing with any move is to have a good story to tell at your next interview. Employers might ask you why you want a new job or why you left your last job. If you can tell a convincing and, ideally, mostly true story no-one will be too worried.

On the other hand, if you are happy in your job and learning lots of new things you can probably take a bit of a holiday from job searching. However, don't get too comfortable! Once you've been there for about a year you should start having a look around. Reviewing some job adverts and looking at what you can apply for is a really good way to think about what your labour market value is. It will also help you to see what other kinds of opportunities are out there that you might now be able to apply for.

Once you've been in a job for a couple of years you should think carefully about whether it is offering you the career development that you want. Some companies tend to promote from within, while others tend to bring in people from outside. A key decision you will have to make is whether there are better opportunities in your current company than you would find outside.

Obviously you don't always have to be climbing the corporate ladder. You may decide that you want to stay in the job that you are doing for a while. This is fine, but you should make this decision from a position of strength. Find out what your options are and then make your decision.

How do I make the most of my experience?

Whatever you have been doing for the first few months after you graduate will have given you some new experiences and helped to develop your understanding of the workplace. You should make the most of this experience by spending some time thinking about what you have learned and how you are going to articulate it to any future employers.

In Chapter 7 we talked about STAR as a way to present your experience on applications and interviews.

S = Situation – What was happening?

T = Task – What needed to be done?

A = Action – What did you do?

R = Result – What happened as a result (and would you do it differently next time)?

Once you have been working for a while you will find that this approach is even more useful. When you were a student you had to think creatively about how you were going to make your experiences on your course, part-time jobs and extra-curricular activities relevant to the world of work. Now that you have some real work experience you have a lot more to draw on.

What's new with you?

Once you've been working for a few months spend a bit of time reflecting on your experience so far. Take the time to write some notes in response to the following questions.

- What have you liked about your first few months at work?
- What have you not liked?
- What have you learned?
- What do you think that you still need to learn?
- What skills do you have now that you didn't have when you graduated?
- How has your network changed? Who do you know that might be helpful to your career?
- How has working changed your ideas about your career?
- If you had your time over again what would you do differently?

Remember, this is just another stop on your journey

When you are at university it is easy to get very excited about your first graduate job. In this book we've been encouraging you to put a lot of work into your career and to find the best job that you can. But it is also important to remember that this is just another stop on your career journey. You have probably changed your ideas about your career a hundred times as you have gone through school, college and university. Now that you are working you should expect to keep changing and developing. As you find out more about yourself and more about work you will keep changing your ideas and aspirations. This is not a problem, in fact we'd be worried if you didn't keep thinking and changing.

IN A NUTSHELL

- It is very easy to end up doing nothing immediately after you graduate. You should recognise this situation quickly and do something purposeful about it.
- It is very common for people to end up in non-graduate jobs. This doesn't have to be a problem; you can move on or, in some cases, craft the job into something that is at graduate level.
- People don't always enjoy their first graduate job. This is normal. You need to show some resilience, but also take steps to improve your situation.
- No-one will be surprised if you change jobs quickly, but try not to hop jobs every month.
- Once you've been in a job for a year or so you should start looking around. This doesn't mean that you have to move, but at least you will know what is out there.

CONCLUSION – FINAL THOUGHTS

This book acts as a guide for students and graduates who are thinking about what they might want to do after university. We have taken a journey from the very beginnings of thinking about you and your career, stopping along the way for some practical application and interview tips and ending up with thoughts on starting your first graduate job and what to do if it doesn't all quite go to plan.

During this process we have tried to distil some wisdom about career management and learning. We have argued that you will need to use your career management skills throughout your life. It's not just about looking for your next job. It's about thinking about what makes you tick and what might help you to feel purposeful, satisfied and fulfilled.

There can be a lot of pressure on students to feel that they ought to have a particular type of job as soon as they leave university. Sometimes this pressure can feel overwhelming and lead to panicked applications, poor choices and disappointment. The guidance in this book has tried to emphasise that your career development is not a separate thing from you, your life and your university experience. It is happening right here, right now, whether you are engaged with it or not. We have also argued that if you devote time to thinking about where you are headed and what you want to do you are likely to be healthier, wealthier and happier.

Things won't always work out as you move from university to work. In fact life and work don't give anyone any guarantees. When things don't go well it can impact on how you feel about yourself and on your overall happiness and well-being. But if you prepare well, actively manage your career and do your best to be resilient in the face of adversity, you've got a pretty good chance that things will work out for you. So keep trying, keep reflecting, keep experimenting and keep learning.

We will leave you with some final thoughts from each section of this book.

1. **I just don't know what to do with myself**
   Your career journey starts with YOU. You should always begin by thinking about who you are, what you like and don't like, your values and talents. Continue to return to this as you re-think your life plan at different stages.

2. **Making the most of your degree**
   Studying for a degree can be challenging and rewarding. In addition to learning a lot about your academic subject you'll be developing a long list of transferable skills and getting to know more about yourself. Take time to think about what you have really learned in your time at university.

3. **Are you experienced?**
   While you are at university you have a wealth of opportunities at your fingertips, so put some time into doing something new. You might surprise yourself and your friends and family with your hidden talents. Remember that work experience can be a road test for a career option, and make the most of the experiences you have.

4. **It's not what you know, it's who you know**
   Use your networks to help you learn about jobs and gain work experience. Get connected online and in person – you never know who is going to be relevant to your career two, five or even ten years down the line.

5. **Look before you leap**
   Treat your job search as if it were an important research assignment. Find out all that you can about the position, company and industry. If you like what you find, then use your knowledge to write impactful applications and to impress at interviews.

6. **Should I stay or should I go?**
   Give further study a chance – but make sure that it is for the right reasons. A Masters degree could help you get a job in some specific industries, but many employers will value work experience just as (or more) highly.

7. **Applications, assessment centres and interviews**
   Prepare to do well in recruitment activities. With good preparation and a friendly proof-reader you can shine from your CV to your assessment centre day.

8. **Help me!**
   Recognising when you would benefit from help demonstrates that you are self-aware and strategic – which happen to be qualities that employers value. As a student or recent graduate you have a long list of support services available to you. Make use of them to help you succeed.

9. **The importance of plan B**

   Life doesn't come with any guarantees. Be prepared for things to change and have a back-up plan at the ready.

10. **Starting work**

    Starting a new job can be stressful and exciting at the same time. Spend some time preparing for your first day. Work hard, listen well and reflect on your workplace behaviour. This will leave a good impression which will pay dividends in the future.

11. **If at first you don't succeed ...**

    Remember that the wrong job is just one stop along the way to the right job (and there will be more than just one right job!). If you don't like how your career is going, it is in your hands to change it.

Remember, career management is for life – give it the attention and love it deserves!

ENDNOTES

i.   Rumsfeld, D. H. (2002). DOD News Briefing. Available from http://archive.defense.gov/Transcripts/Transcript.aspx?TranscriptID=2636 [Accessed 3 July 2016].

ii.   Kolb, D. A. (1984). *Experiential Learning: Experience as the Source of Learning and Development.* New Jersey: Prentice-Hall.

iii.   Taylor, A. R. and Hooley, T. (2014). Evaluating the impact of career management skills module and internship programme within a university business school. *British Journal of Guidance & Counselling,* 42(5): 487–99.

iv.   Blustein, D. L. (2006). *The Psychology of Working: A New Perspective for Career Development, Counseling, and Public Policy.* Mahwah, NJ: Lawrence Erlbaum Associates.

v.   Granovetter, M. (1973). The strength of weak ties. *American Journal of Sociology,* 78(6): 1360–80.

vi.   For example, see Gupta, A. and Bennett, S. E. (2014). An empirical analysis of the effect of MBA programs on organizational success. *International Journal of Educational Management,* 28(4), 451–60.

vii.   Ratcliff, R. (2014). Will doing a masters get you a better job? Well, maybe …, *Guardian,* www.theguardian.com/education/2014/apr/14/will-doing-masters-get-you-better-job.

viii.   Artes, J., Ball, C., Forbes, P. and Hughes, T. (2014). *Taught Postgraduate Employability and Employer Engagement: Masters with a Purpose.* Manchester: HECSU.

ix.   Hooley, T., Bright, J. and Winter, D. (2016). *You're Hired! Job Hunting Online: The Complete Guide.* Bath: Trotman.

x.   Roderick, C. and Meachin, J. (2010). *You're Hired! Psychometric Tests: Proven Tactics to Help You Pass.* Bath: Trotman.

xi.   For more information on the Destinations of Leavers in Higher Education survey visit www.hefce.ac.uk/lt/dlhe.

xii.   Mavromaras, K., McGuinness, S., O'Leary, N., Sloane, P. and Wei, Z. (2013). Job mismatches and labour market outcomes: panel evidence on university graduates. *Economic Record,* 89 (286), 382–95.

xiii. Elias, P. and Purcell, K. (2013). *Classifying Graduate Occupations for the Knowledge Society*. Coventry: Institute for Employment Research, University of Warwick.

xiv. Tovey, A. (2014). Why do 1 in 4 graduates quit within a year of starting work? *Daily Telegraph*. Available from www.telegraph.co.uk/finance/jobs/11045445/Why-do-1-in-4-graduates-quit-within-a-year-of-starting-work.html [Accessed 5 February 2017].